Let God Be God

MICHAEL FORSTER was born in 1946, the son of an Anglican priest. Most of his working life was spent as a music teacher, until in 1986 he entered Regent's Park College, Oxford, to train for the Baptist Ministry. He was ordained in 1989, and, following a period in church-based ministry, he now divides his time between writing and working as a Free Church Chaplain with Leicestershire Mental Health Services.

Let God Be God

An encouragement
to grow in faith

Michael
Forster

Kevin
Mayhew

First published in 1995 by
KEVIN MAYHEW LTD
Rattlesden
Bury St Edmunds
Suffolk IP30 0SZ

ISBN 0 86209 650 2
Catalogue No 1500026

Cover design by Veronica Ward
and Graham Johnstone

Editor: Alison Sommazzi
Typesetting and Page Creation by Vicky Brown
Printed and bound in Great Britain

FOREWORD

Is it possible to have faith in an objectively living God as we approach the twenty-first century: in the face not only of scientific advances but of the sheer inexcusable ghastliness of much that happens in the world, can we still believe in a loving, personal God? That question, while admittedly far from new, is becoming more urgent in the world as it is. I believe it is possible to sustain such a belief, but no one ever said it would be easy, or no one worth listening to, anyway. Although in these pages I pose some hard questions and find it necessary to move away from what many regard as 'traditional' ideas, I find myself still able to affirm belief in a personal God; still able, however inadequately I myself may do it, to live by faith. The basic challenge is to move from believing in a God who is in control of the minutiae of daily life to trusting one who works by relationship and the persuasive power of love.

If that basic shift of perspective is made, questions are then raised about other aspects of faith. What *is* 'faith'? What is the standing and the value of scripture? Most importantly of all, what kind of God makes any sort of sense in the present context? These and other questions must also be pursued if our faith is to be something by which we can genuinely live. While the book makes no attempt to cover every eventuality – to unravel the mysteries of the Trinity or to present a doctrine of the Holy Spirit, for example – it does attempt to grapple seriously with the fundamental issues which religious belief has to confront. God is eternal mystery, and we must never expect everything to be plain and simple; and yet we are rational beings, and faith should not require that we suspend our reason. My concern, therefore, is to address that fundamental question and to do it in as readable a way as possible.

This is a book written on the move, in the hope of encouraging others who wish to make the journey. It began with a carefully laid out plan which plotted each step in the journey in fairly close detail, and which very soon had to be abandoned. That is how it is on a journey of faith: we cannot begin by saying where we intend to finish up, but only step into the unknown, hoping, trusting, believing that God is there and has some sort of direction in mind.

I make no promises that this will be comfortable reading, but I believe it points the way to a faith which not only is sustainable in the present age but which offers the hope of life in all its fullness both now and in the unknown that is ahead of us all.

MICHAEL FORSTER

ACKNOWLEDGEMENTS: I am indebted to a number of people for invaluable help in the preparation of this book. I cannot possibly name everyone whose encouragement I have valued and whose insights I have plundered, but a few must be singled out for particular mention:

Brian Tucker for his initial encouragement and insights.

John Weaver for reading the first draft and finding room for encouragement as well as invaluable criticism.

Beryl Johnson for undertaking the proof reading.

I must also express my debt in more general terms to the tutorial staff of Regent's Park College, Oxford, who between 1986 and 1989 shared with me the journey which, as it turned out, prepared me for the task of writing this book.

The author and publishers wish to thank the following for permission to reproduce copyright material:

HarperCollins Publishers, 77-78 Fulham Palace Road, Hammersmith, London W6 8JB for extracts from *Eternal Life* by Hans Kung (Collins 1984).

National Council of Churches of Christ in the USA for scripture quotations which are taken from the Revised Standard Version of the Bible © 1946, 1952, 1971 by the Division of Christian Education of the National Council of the Churches of Christ in the USA.

Regent's Park College, Pusey Street, Oxford OX1 2LB for extracts from *In the Beginning God* by John D. Weaver (Regent's Study Guides 1994).

SCM Press Ltd, 26-30 Tottenham Road, London N1 4BZ for extracts from *The Incarnation of Freedom and Love* by Ruth Page (SCM Press 1991), *The Prophets Vol 1* by Klaus Koch (SCM Press 1982), *The Power of the Poor in History* by Gustavo Gutierrez (SCM Press 1983), *From God in Creation* by Jurgen Mottmann (SCM Press 1985) and *Principles of Christian Theology* by John Macquarrie (SCM Press 1986).

SPCK, Holy Trinity Church, Marylebone Road, London NW1 4DU for extracts from *Science and Christian Belief* by John Polkinghorne (SPCK 1994).

To Jean

Contents

CHAPTER ONE

LET GOD BE GOD

He said to him, '" You shall love the Lord your God
with all your heart, and with all your soul,
and with all your mind."'[1]

The call to love God with all our mind seems to imply that the intellect which God has given us is not to be excluded from our faith; to do so would be to love God with less than the whole of our being. We do not want to turn faith into an intellectual exercise, of course, but if it is to be genuine faith, a matter we shall discuss further in the next chapter, then clearly we cannot and must not shirk the hard questions. Indeed, my own experience is that if we try to do so we miss out on most of the real 'hidden treasure' which Jesus described as the kingdom of God. So we need to ask what kind of God we may believe in and indeed whether belief in a supernatural God is possible at all as we approach the twenty-first century. If our faith and our God are real, we have nothing to fear from such questions. If they are not, then the sooner we find out and start to centre our lives upon something more helpful, the better.

We are now in some difficulty as to how to proceed. How are we to know God? It should be said, of course, that if God is indeed supernatural then we cannot study him as we would any natural phenomenon. God does not sit quietly on a laboratory bench while we prod him, peer through microscopes at him and dissect him in the preparation of learned papers. Some would say we can only learn of God through his own revelation in scripture, where he chooses to reveal himself; we must not rely upon our own feelings or

[1] Matt 22:37

experiences. The trouble is that when we start to read scripture we inevitably read it through the tinted lenses of our own experiences, feelings, prejudices and partially formed ideas, and the very nature of the Bible (which we shall discuss more in Chapter 3) makes such a process unavoidable. Others would contend – with considerable justification – that the only way to understand God is through his *incarnate* Word: Jesus. This is a powerful argument, and one with which I have considerable sympathy. However, the same cautionary note still applies: our understanding of Jesus – like our reading of scripture – can be highly subjective as religious and political history has shown.

The short answer to all this is that our knowledge of God is developed through a combination of things: principally, our experiences, our own personalities, scripture and our analysis of the world around us, each of which influences the others. So we end up with a circle; a kind of chicken and egg situation. The more I discuss these things with people – Christians and others – the more convinced I am that in practice we tend to begin from a basic idea about what God must be, and our particular approach to scripture and faith as a whole springs largely from that. How we read scripture will depend very much upon this basic idea (however subconscious) of God which we have when we begin. So it seems reasonable to try to break into the circle at that point.

First, however, it is worth thinking a little about the general approach. What we are about to do may well appear threatening, but I believe it is necessary if faith in God is to grow. I also firmly believe that the rewards more than justify the risk, as the following story may illustrate.

Methodology: Foundations and Structures

An important moment in my own journey happened – appropriately enough – on a train. It was the spring of 1987 somewhere between Oxford and Wolverhampton. The Inter-City train was making good time, but my thoughts were racing faster.

I was in the early stages of a theological training course which would lead to ordination. Having always thought of myself as an open-minded liberal, I had approached the course with a confidence which needed and deserved to be shattered. I had been warned that I would find the questions threatening, but had thought that that only really applied to others; those narrow-minded people whom, having so labelled them, I could dismiss from my thoughts.

So I was surprised to find myself, on the train journey home, wondering whether I should continue to ask the questions which had been forced upon me by the book I was reading. Eventually I decided it had been a hard session, and I should be justified in putting off consideration of the whole matter until another time. I was now returning home, and to the church which I served as 'student minister'; I could lose myself in the practicalities of urban ministry for a while.

Accordingly, next morning I turned up for a site meeting at the stripped-out shell of our church building, which was being renovated; I was to meet the architect and other experts to review the work which would eventually include the installation of a baptistry large enough for total immersion. When I went into the building, I saw to my horror that there was a hole about twelve inches wide directly under the base of a main wall. Daylight was gleefully streaming through it into the building and, as far as I was concerned, was not welcome. I quickly found the architect and asked him whether he was trying to destroy the place, and why. Very patiently, he explained that the foundations needed strengthening. 'If you put a baptistry in there as it is,' he said, 'the pressure of the concrete will push the wall out. So we're taking the foundations out bit by bit and pumping in vibrated concrete.'

The light dawned.

The building was old, and was now going to be asked to fulfil a purpose which the original designers had not anticipated. While in sound enough condition structurally, it could no longer meet the needs of the day. So it had to be altered. The problem then was that the foundations which, like the structure, had been quite adequate for many years, were no longer up to the job and needed to be strengthened. So a new element was to be introduced: vibrated concrete – a material quite foreign to the original builders. And before this could be done, we had to take what seemed to me to be an enormous risk. We had to dig away at the very foundations of the building, and undermine (albeit temporarily) that on which its existence depended. It was a very vulnerable feeling, rather akin to that which I had experienced the previous evening.

My faith had rested on certain foundations. I should never have described myself as a fundamentalist, but there were some things which seemed indispensable. It had never occurred to me that *they* would be questioned. The problem was, did I have sufficient faith in the Architect to allow the process to go on? I had two choices. That was one of them. The other was to shout, 'Stop!' I could perhaps leave things as they were; if I kept those fundamental things in place, and refused to let them be tampered with, then I might – just might – hope that my faith would not crumble. But it would not grow, either. I should be left with a structure which had been quite adequate in the past, but would not now meet the needs. Furthermore, I would always know that there were questions, and as time went on, the structure might come under new pressures for which the foundations were not designed. What would I then do? This was now made inevitable, because I had glimpsed those questions, and would always know that I had shirked them. Inevitably, they would haunt me and perhaps destroy this carefully preserved but inadequate faith.

I took a decision, not merely to ask the threatening questions, but to keep on asking them, and to follow through the supplementary ones. This was not because I now had very much confidence in myself – that had been well and truly exposed for the fraud it had been – but because I had seen something more important, more fundamental than that. If God was truly God, then ultimately no question could be too hard. And if he was not, then I had better find out sooner rather than later.

I also realised that this is a call which has been constantly before the people of God. We are always and everywhere being called out of slavery. As the Israelites found out, the certainty of 'Egypt'[2] is tempting. It may be limiting, but it is *safe.* The desert is best avoided. Similarly, to return to the other metaphor, the ancient monuments of the past may not be very useful now, but at least they are still there. Trendy new ideas might come and go, but as long as we retain the foundations of our ancient faith, we shall always have somewhere safe to retreat to, away from the terrors of the present and the uncertainty of the future.

It is not difficult to trace this process throughout the history of Christianity. One example will do for now. When scientists first began to intimate that they thought the world might be a sphere, the Church had palpitations. And the palpitations grew into a full-blown heart attack when the ludicrous idea seemed to be gaining acceptance. Why, the whole structure of the faith rested upon belief in a flat earth. Without that, where was heaven? More importantly for some, where was hell? So many stories in scripture depended on the idea of God 'up there', and if he was not 'up there', then where was he? What was to be made of the ascension story? This whole idea of a round earth, now as certain as anything can be, seemed then to put the very existence of Christendom in jeopardy. And yet Christianity has survived. This particular bit of the foundations turned out to be quite dispensable *as long as it was replaced with something else.* And so theologians turned their attention more carefully to the ideas which had seemed so cut and dried before, and found richer, deeper, more powerful truths in them.

This, then, is the kind of process which goes on in microcosm in our individual lives. It would seem ridiculous now for the Church to be stolidly maintaining that the earth

[2] e. g. Exodus 14:11

was flat. It seems equally ridiculous to think that the authenticity of Christianity, even the very existence of God, once seemed threatened by this. The faith has grown in new ways to meet new circumstances, just as did the church building which now serves its community in new ways, and has come to represent life and hope to many more people; all because an architect was prepared to take the risk of digging out its foundations.

That is what has to happen in our lives. Many people are now finding that the traditional structures of the faith are inadequate. They do not meet current needs and indeed do not even seem viable in current circumstances. But people are afraid to renovate them, in case the foundations prove inadequate. There is only one answer: we have to trust the architect. The only alternative is either to continue with something which we know is inadequate until such time as it falls apart of its own accord, or to abandon it completely.

I can say that in my experience God has proved more than worthy of that trust. It has been a threatening and sometimes excruciatingly painful business, but without exception I have come through each new set of questions with a firmer, not weaker, faith. The superstructure now looks remarkably different from before, and still remarkably similar. Likewise, the foundations have certainly changed, but maintain their continuity with the past.

More importantly, I am convinced that the kind of faith I had at an earlier stage of my life could not have met my needs since, and especially in the more recent years. Had I not been enabled to begin the journey on which I am now embarked, I think I should probably have found it impossible to maintain any kind of religious commitment. However, I should not so easily use the past tense. The journey, and the digging, both continue. In many ways, I have fewer 'answers' now than I had then. If I can claim to 'know' any more than I used to, it is that – even though there may not be immediate answers – it's alright to ask the questions. God is indeed big enough to take it. More than that, he actually wants us to do it so that we may grow in our relationship with him. When the foundations are dug away, it may be difficult to realise that anything can replace them, but in my experience there is always something; something better, stronger, more life-giving than was there before. Something which meets the needs I have now and does not ask me to stop the journey and live in the past.

So, before moving on, allow me to repeat that I write all this from a position of belief. That is, I believe in God as living, and objectively real. I believe that he, and his purpose, have been made known in the person of Jesus, and that commitment to that God is the way to life in all its fullness.

In what follows, we shall be examining closely the foundations of many important things. I shall suggest that some parts need to be replaced but, like the architect in the story, we shall only remove a little at a time and at each stage replace it with something which I believe is stronger and more life-enhancing.

So let the work commence.

The Nature of God

'Sin is the refusal to let God be God.'[3] So wrote Gerard Hughes. The problem is that any concept of God at all is bound, by definition, to be inadequate. God would not be God if he could be contained in neat and tidy compartments which suited the size of our minds. So any attempt to define God will be in danger of being sinful. This is what many great theologians and philosophers have rightly feared who have argued that God is unknowable. They are cautioning us against the danger of thinking that we have everything worked out, and they echo the warning given to Moses when he asked for a quick definition:

> God said to Moses, 'I AM WHO I AM. This is what you are to say to the Israelites: "I AM has sent me to you."'[4]

[3] Gerard Hughes: *God of Surprises* (DLT 1985 p. 77)
[4] Ex. 3:14

This could also be read, 'I will be what I will be.' It is for God, not for us, to say who and what he will be, and he refuses to be narrowly defined by a label. Moses is to portray him as transcendent Mystery. However, this is not to say, as some have tried to say, that we should not seek to know God. That would be a ludicrous idea, since the Bible itself actually claims to reveal him. What it does say is that we should never think we have the ultimate definition. As soon as we think that, we are idolators, for we have committed ourselves to love, worship and obey something which is less than God. In taking our partial understanding and regarding it as the whole, we are refusing to let God be God for us.

One early attempt to define God is found in a prayer by Anselm which addresses God as *That Than Which Nothing Greater Can Be Conceived* (which may be conveniently shortened to 'TTWNGCBC'). That seems like a reasonable definition of God, but of course we still have to decide what we mean by greatness. The definition has even been used to 'prove' the existence of God, on the basis that it is greater to exist than not to exist! This illustrates the kind of circular argument which characterises a lot of theological thinking. We begin by defining God, and then use that definition to prove whatever we want to prove. Let us imagine asking a number of different people to describe God on the basis of that definition. A soldier would probably speak in terms of a great warrior or military leader; society has too long suffered from that image of God and still suffers from it today. A politician might define God as someone who could get his policies accepted, or who could persuade people to believe (in) him. A rock music or football fan would think in terms of a star performer, and a baby – were it able to speak – would probably say that God was a well-filled breast.

So the definition is of little use on its own, but is far from redundant; we might use it as a springboard to consider the possibilities. It really hinges upon what we think it means to be 'great', or 'The Greatest'.

The God who intervenes

British Gas once used an advertising slogan which ran, 'Don't you just love being in control?' For many people, to call God 'TTWNGCBC' means just that: that he is supremely 'in control'. This sounds reasonable enough on the surface; how could anyone who is not in control of things be regarded as God at all? So long as God is *in control*, we can face whatever the present holds, knowing that all will be well in the end. We may even say that any present difficulties we experience are part of the great mysterious plan. Recently, when embarking upon a change of career, I was assured by a number of people that I was bound to succeed because what I was doing was right, and God would be *in control* of my life. A number of years ago, this would have caused me no problems. In fact I made the same claim in retrospect when I was a music student. There had been a number of coincidences, including last-minute changes of plan by other people, which had led to my going to music college rather than to teacher training college. I had never really thought that I was music college material, and as I look back I think that I was right. Perhaps that was another reason why I was inclined to see divine manipulation of events in what had happened. In fact, as I later realised, this was a simplistic view. Who knows what course my life might have taken had that specific sequence of events not occurred? It might not have meant total failure; music might not have been the only possible course for me at that time. Perhaps, in fact, a slight change in the pattern could have sent me into an equally satisfying career in law, or politics or medicine – who knows? I now believe that I had followed one of a number of possible routes, simply responding to events as they happened. I cannot now honestly think that I struggled my way through a career in music teaching thanks to the manipulation of events by a God who could at least as easily – and more honestly – have given me the ability to do it on my own merits.

There are various problems with the idea of God being 'in control' in the way people generally mean. We often hear stories similar to my own of 'miracles' where it appears that the world has been reordered for the specific benefit of one person. This kind of manipulation raises enormous questions, some of which carry serious implications. We shall be discussing the subject of miracles in more detail later; here we are primarily concerned with the nature of God.

Firstly, we must ask: what kind of relationship does God have with his creation? Is any good relationship manipulative? We know manipulative people who will claim to have the best interests of their families or friends at heart, and most of us accept (at least where other people's relationships are concerned) that 'you have to love people enough to let them go'. We also recognise in human relationships that love must be freely accepted and freely given, if it is to be real love. Both parties must be free to accept or reject it. Does God want a genuine free response from creation, or is he willing to accept second best by manipulating it? So we must ask whether a God who claimed to want freedom for and relationship with us, and yet manipulated creation (even for our benefit), would be the greatest that could be conceived.

There is also the question of human responsibility. God really cannot have it both ways; he cannot manipulate us when it suits him to do so and then hold us responsible for our own lives. Either we are responsible people or we are puppets. An example of this occurred in a sermon I once heard in which the preacher told us how, when he was late for a train because the road was blocked by an accident, God had delayed the train to enable him to catch it. I have no doubt that the train was delayed – that is hardly an unusual phenomenon – but to attribute the event to divine intervention begs a number of questions. If we are going to an important appointment then we are normally responsible enough to allow for the unexpected. We know traffic jams can occur for many reasons, and we allow plenty of time. We also accept that part of the risk of living in society, and not being cut off from it, is that other people's misfortunes will sometimes affect us. Of all religious people, Christians especially should not expect to be shielded from that.

But there are more basic questions. We have to ask about God's values. He will apparently delay a train full of people, some of whom may also have been late for appointments elsewhere, for the sake of one specially favoured individual. (Perhaps the interpretation of this event as a miracle says more about the subject's sense of his own importance than it does about God . . .) The question we should be asking, of course, is why God so often seems to go about things in an arbitrary and chaotic manner. In this particular instance, why did he not simply prevent the accident which caused the hold up? It seems we are dealing with a God neither of order nor of compassion. Furthermore, while apparently quite ready to interfere with creation's freedom so as to prevent a little embarrassment or a lost business deal, God seems to be unwilling to do so in order to prevent tens of thousands of children from dying of war, disease and malnutrition every day. The traditional answer to this objection is that God is unknowable, and his ways are higher than ours, but this really will not do. Those who say this claim that this 'unknowable' God has made himself known in scripture and, with definitive finality, in Jesus. Indeed, God has made very clear to us throughout scripture the kind of value we are to place upon people, and any of us who were prepared to ignore the death of even one individual if we had the power to stop it, but are unwilling to be late for an appointment, would get scant support from the God revealed in scripture. Unless God is a hypocrite, he must himself abide by the standards he sets us. We are therefore entitled – required – to ask questions such as this.

Here of course we have touched upon the fundamental flaw in this concept of a manipulative God. He must be responsible for evil. Whatever is said about Satan, a God who is willing and able to manipulate creation must bear the ultimate responsibility for its condition. Unless we are suggesting that Satan is an eternal reality (a thoroughly heretical idea by any standards) we must ask about his origins, and why he is apparently allowed to wreak havoc in the world. How careless of God, having made the world perfect, to allow this lesser force to corrupt it. The traditional belief about Satan as a 'fallen angel' founders on the very rocks on which it attempts to find refuge. If Lucifer was an angel, in heaven, where no evil can enter, how did he come to fall in the first place?

The answer must be that this mythical character, Satan, is a useful metaphor for all kinds of things but, in the end, that is all it is. It certainly cannot be used to explain away the responsibility of an all-powerful God for the state of his creation. To use free will as the catch-all response will not do either. The whole idea of a God who intervenes compromises free will anyway. If creation is being manipulated to fulfil some predetermined master plan, then freedom of any kind is illusory. So why does God not admit the fact and be honest about it? If he can interfere with the free will of a railway company to fulfil its contractual obligations, why did he not interfere with Lucifer's free will in the first place and save himself and us a lot of grief?

This brings us to the most fundamental objection. God is said by most religions to be the only source of meaning for creation. If that is the case, it is strange that he should be the cause of its meaninglessness. The claim that God is in fact moving things along a predetermined path to a conclusion planned before time began empties our own individual lives of meaning. If creation will eventually be as God has already decided, then whatever we do can make no difference to that, one way or the other. There is no contribution for us to make to creation, and our life is meaningless. This is made all the more monstrous, of course, by God's apparent pretence to the contrary. It seems that he leads us to believe that we are partners in creation, and that we are of eternal significance, when nothing could be further from the truth. A God who treats – uses – people in that way is certainly not *That Than Which Nothing Greater Can Be Conceived.*

If this has been the accepted model of God (and if my objections to it are largely accepted) then I have dug a hole beneath the foundations of faith. With what can that hole be filled? There are a number of possible materials, of which I shall consider two. The first, although it may appear the most obvious, is not in my opinion the best; but it is becoming more widely accepted, and we need to examine it.

The God who is All in the Mind

Some thinkers, aware of the kind of objections I have outlined above, have concluded that there can be no place for belief in an interventionist God in the present world, and have gone on from there to argue that there can therefore be no place for God at all, except as a useful concept. The idea of an objectively existing God, they argue, is not only a violation of reason; it ultimately demeans and enslaves humanity.

I have no difficulty in accepting that the existence of God cannot be proved, and in fact find much which is helpful in the Christian humanist position. Furthermore, I would agree that the narrowly defined 'God' proclaimed by a large number of people is responsible for horrendous evils. People have killed for it, have bought and sold others in its name, and have been induced to throw away beautifully creative lives in misguided sacrifice to it. I do not believe in that God, and if I did would certainly not worship it – except perhaps out of totally understandable fear.

The case made by those who believe in God as a concept, rather than objective reality, is that God is a human creation. In earlier, less scientific times, people needed to find explanations for things which were beyond their understanding and, precisely because they did not understand the universe, built up systems of beliefs which now simply do not stand up. We know that we do not live in a three-tier universe with God at the top, hell at the bottom and a flat earth in between. Therefore, much of the imagery which was so helpful to earlier generations causes problems for us. We have to accept that it *is* imagery. It is easy and logical, although by no means necessary in my view, to go on from there to declare that *all* ideas of God are only imagery, of purely human creation, and that it is impossible to believe in an objectively existing God.

If this proposition is accepted, then a process of reorientation begins in one's thinking. 'God' becomes a helpful metaphor for all that is good. It may be used to refer to the essential goodness in creation, or to the better instincts in humanity. We may still say 'I believe in God', because we do; it is just that we understand the word differently. This process can be applied to all other Christian doctrines; lack of space precludes a full treatment here, but we can look at a few examples.

- Jesus can still be God for us, in that he had a deep affinity with this essential goodness we call God, and showed us how to live by that, rather than our less healthy inclinations. He embodied 'God'. He was 'God' incarnate.

- On this understanding, resurrection does not mean that Jesus' body literally rose from the dead, but his disciples were clearly so inspired by him that he continued to live on in their lives and became such a powerful inspiration for them that the only way of describing it was the symbolic language of 'resurrection'. The image is very powerful today in proclaiming hope of renewal even in the most dire human circumstances. Even the death of our bodies (and our conscious selves) does not mean the end of our personal significance.

- Eternal life (again, on this understanding) ceases to mean individual survival and means instead that the lives we live here and now may

> have eternal significance because of what we contribute to creation, the more so if we live Christlike lives.

In many ways, I have no difficulty with any of this. Indeed, there are various aspects of this interpretation which can (in my view must) also be part of traditional beliefs, and it is obviously not necessary to abandon the conventional interpretation in order to see the symbolism. All Christian doctrines have many layers of meaning, reaching profound depths of symbolism, and an over-adherence to literalism has certainly impoverished the faith and made it meaningless to a large number of people. There is no problem with the conceptual understanding of God, from this point of view. I just do not happen to believe that it is necessary to throw out the baby with the bathwater.

Of course, if it were really a choice between the crudely manipulative God of fundamentalist testimony and the purely conceptual understanding, then many of us would prefer the latter. Indeed we should have no choice since we find the former quite without credibility. In point of fact, though, there are many ways into the mystery of God, and a multitude of understandings, most of which (including the two above) have something to offer and all of which are incomplete. I propose to offer one; one which I find believable and healthy; one which seems to me to be at least as consistent with biblical teaching as any other and to which I am prepared to commit myself in faith.

The God who Relates

We have seen the problems with the image of a God who is, in the simple sense, 'in control', but a God who is *not* in control seems like a contradiction – and a terrifying one at that. It need not be so, indeed quite the contrary. The invitation is to be believe not in a God who is powerless to control, but a God who is so great that he does not *need* to be in constant control. Such a God may freely choose to relinquish that kind of control in order to enable relationships to grow; relationships of a kind and a quality that could never be built unless both parties were free. Free will is an accepted part of traditional Christian doctrine, but is often used as a simplistic explanation for evil, rather than given serious consideration. If that consideration is given, it soon becomes clear that our freedom is necessary if our relationship with God is to be genuine. It also becomes clear, but is less easy to accept, that for God to take our freedom seriously means that he limits his own freedom to intervene.

Perhaps an example would help here. A vivid memory from my childhood is of a seaside holiday at which my father spent what was, in terms of his own income, an enormous amount of money on a toy yacht. I was of course delighted with the unexpected gift, and knew I had to take great care of it, since there would certainly be no possibility of replacing it should it be lost or damaged. Then one morning we were out on the sea in a dinghy, with my toy yacht bobbing on the waves beside us as my father held on to it by means of a piece of string. I knew of course that the yacht was safe. I trusted my father completely, and knew that he would never let it go. Imagine my reaction when he proposed doing precisely that! Such an idea was inconceivable on that vast, rolling sea and I naturally resisted, not wanting to lose my precious toy. Eventually, however, I was persuaded that it would be quite safe, since in our vessel we could always catch up with it. It could not get out of our reach.

I cannot adequately describe in words the difference it made to see the toy actually floating free. It took on a completely different significance. No longer was it a plaything, but it was in a sense real. To see it riding freely on the waves produced a feeling of near-euphoria. More than that: my admiration of my father increased immeasurably. I had known that he was quite capable of holding onto the string, but now it seemed that even this great ocean could not defeat him. Why, the man was positively omnipotent! Of course he did not need neurotically to hang onto the bit of string; he was much greater than that.

Very well then. The invitation being offered is to believe in a God so great that he *does not need* to be 'in control' in the sense in which we usually understand that expression. He has such confidence in his power that he can set his creation free, knowing that not even the greatest sea of chaos will ever be able to put us out of his reach. If God is *That Than Which Nothing Greater Can Be Conceived,* he must have sufficient confidence in his powers to let creation be free. More than that: if he is infinite love, then he must actually want creation to be truly free. I said that I experienced a sensation of euphoria seeing this most precious toy actually set free. The toy became 'real'. What we need to learn is that the demand for a God who is 'in control' is really more to do with our own sense of insecurity than anything about God – just as my desire that my father keep hold of the string was really a sign of my lack of trust in him. He proved more than trustworthy. In the same way, if we are prepared to allow God to set us free on what has been called 'the Sea of Faith'[5], then we can experience the joy of no longer being 'toys' but becoming 'real'. This involves risk and responsibility. Perhaps being a toy is safer, less demanding, but in the end it is totally unfulfilling. If we are to be real people, then we must let God be God.

Sin is the refusal to let God be God. The God in constant control of the minutiae of day-to-day life is in my submission an idol, and the worship of such a god is therefore sinful. What are the consequences of that sin? Let us return to the analogy and suppose that I had flatly refused to let my father release the string. Suppose that I had made my fear so obvious that he had abandoned his idea. One of the most memorable experiences of my childhood would have been forfeit. We should never have had the thrill of seeing the yacht go free. The toy would never have become 'real'. If we insist upon the idolatry of a god who neurotically holds the string, we deny God the joy of seeing us truly set free, and we

[5] The title of a book by Don Cupitt, and the name of a movement pursuing lines of thinking arising from it.

express the desire to be mere toys rather than real people. In daily life we may well meet people who nurture such a desire and who will defend to the death this little idol on whom their life depends. What a shame that in their vain attempt to preserve their life, they are losing out on life in all its fullness.[6]

Of course, there is a fundamental inadequacy in the analogy I have used. (Actually there are a number, but one is of particular significance.) The picture we now have is of God riding in a boat on the waters of chaos, keeping track of his free-floating creation. We need to move on from this; it has its uses but, like all images of God, it is inadequate on its own. It simply serves as a starter, to make the point about freedom. When we consider our understanding of God, we need to go further. A better picture is presented by Ruth Page when she points out that, since God is all-powerful and is present everywhere, '. . . all creation must be "in" God. There is nowhere else for it to be.'[7] This is a healthier image by far. Of course it poses philosophical problems, but they are outside the scope of this book. Suffice to say that they are not insuperable and are dealt with very thoroughly by a number of theologians and philosophers. For our purpose it is sufficient to think of the infinite God being able to allow creation ample space and freedom within himself. Thought of in this way, the idea of a God who is not in the traditional sense 'in control' becomes not only acceptable but attractive. We might speak of the distinction between a grip and an embrace. The former is a sign of possession, the latter of love. God does not grasp creation, but embraces it and, being infinite, can do so while allowing it all the space and freedom it could need or desire. Clearly, if this is the relationship between God and creation, we have no need to fear becoming separated from God, and can take the risks of faith, trusting in the God who does not manipulate events for us, but will never desert us either.

[6] cf. Matthew 16:25-27 par.
[7] *The Incarnation of Freedom and Love* (SCM 1991) p.1

If we now return to the ancient definition of God as 'TTWNGCBC', *that than which nothing greater can be conceived*, we find that we can still live with that definition. The difference is that greatness is now defined not in terms of control but of love. If we believe, as I think most of us do, that to love is greater than to control, then we have actually found a possible understanding of God which, even on this basis alone, is better. It lacks all the unhealthy tyrannical, manipulative elements of the *God in control* model, and actually means that the existence of God, far from demeaning humanity (as some philosophers and theologians claim) actually gives it greater meaning since this God has evidently chosen to be God *for us*, rather than making us to be *for him*. This model says that we are not the result of a mere accident, and neither are we the plaything of a cosmic wizard. We have specifically been created as an act of love, with the freedom to accept or reject that love as we choose. And God has done us the honour of saying – and showing – that we are important, essential even, to his happiness – so essential that he will suffer inconceivable pain to keep the relationship with us open. Such a God can hardly be said to demean us.

A Flexible Foundation

In the Bible, a very powerful image is that of the building set upon rock. That image of course is generally very helpful. However, if we lived in San Francisco, for example, we might be a little cautious about pushing the analogy too far. In earthquake zones, architects have learned to build flexibility into the design of buildings – and we are learning that faith can be something of an earthquake zone! Throughout its history, the church has found that too solid a foundation, which allows no 'swayability', can be something of a mixed blessing, if indeed it is a blessing at all. Ever since the Enlightenment (at the very least) the unyielding foundation of belief in a God who is 'in control' of every detail of life has actually been the cause of crumbling faith for many people.

All this, of course, is emphatically not to say that *God* needs to change to keep in fashion, so to speak. I am saying that our own inadequate *understanding* of God must change. We must be ready and able to admit when we – and perhaps others of higher reputation – are holding on to beliefs which no longer work. This is made possible by the belief in a relational God, and that in fact is the God who has, according to Christian belief, been made known to us.

THE GOD REVEALED IN JESUS

We are now face to face with the person at the heart of any specifically Christian theology: the person of Jesus of Nazareth. It is his personality which is definitive for the Christian understanding of God. At this point it would be possible to begin a complete book, just on the subject of Jesus, but that is not my purpose. What is important here is to ask whether the kind of understanding of God which I am trying to communicate is consistent with the revelation in Jesus. I not only believe that it is consistent; I am convinced that the very nature of Christianity requires belief in a relational God, and in a God who limits himself to make that relationship possible. For what do we see in Jesus? Do we see a manipulative personality who set out to impose himself upon creation, to dominate it? That would certainly be the image created by many of the aggressive evangelistic campaigns fashionable in the free market ethos of our modern capitalist culture. But they in themselves are really modelled upon their own culture rather than upon Jesus.

> Today, for instance, one of the models of power is the cohesive organisation of an international conglomerate, with carefully encouraged loyalty from its staff. None of that shows in Jesus. One of the delights of reading the Gospels in an age when managerial and entrepreneurial models of relationship

> proliferate is to find that he was not organised in that sense. He conducted no strategic evangelisation crusade. Instead, he put himself where people of all kinds were and let the encounters come ad hoc.[8]

Ruth Page has identified the essential feature of Jesus' ministry, which was a complete lack of pressure. Urgency, of course, but not coercive pressure. He would not use supernatural powers or spectacular stunts, or the ways of this world to manipulate the response he wanted.[9] Jesus came to be 'for others' – not so that they could be 'for him'. He called those who would to follow him, always leaving the door open for a change of mind. When some of his own disciples decided that his teaching was 'too hard', he did not try to dissuade them from going, but turned to the others and said, 'What about you – will you go as well?'[10] When he was approached by three apparent converts promising lifelong devotion, he spelled out the costs of commitment so graphically that they went away. And he stood, no doubt sadly, and allowed them to do so.[11]

Here is the image of God for us: coming among us, seeking relationship, continually offering love and acceptance, but bending over backwards to allow us complete freedom of response. That freedom even extended to the ability not simply to walk away from Jesus but to slander, ridicule and ultimately to attack, torture and kill him. This is the God who does not need to hang on to the string; who can allow the toys to be real. Here is the image of a God who can *afford* to weaken himself to the point of death and beyond, and who is willing to do so rather than try to force a response. Here is the image of a God who relates, rather than controls. When we come to think about the subject of atonement, and look at the

[8] Ruth Page: *The Incarnation of Freedom and Love* (SCM 1991) p.16
[9] Matt. 4:1-11 and par.
[10] John 6:66-67
[11] Luke 9:57-62

cross in greater depth, I shall be attempting to show that ultimately there is infinitely more power in this weakness than in anything else.

There are many questions still unanswered by all of this, and many which I am not yet in a position to answer. I shall attempt to answer some of those which I can, in the subsequent chapters of this book; whether I do so adequately, the reader must judge. As for those I cannot answer, I can only say that I continue the journey. I might of course be wildly wrong in much of what I believe, but in the end what I believe is all I have. I must live by that, and commit myself to it in all its incompleteness, trusting where I cannot know, and open to the refining influence of what we, from whatever theological standpoint, would commonly call the Spirit of God. In short, I must let God be God for me. That is the only way I can be a person of faith. But what is 'faith'? That is the next question we must explore.

CHAPTER TWO

FAITH AND DOUBT

There lives more faith in honest doubt,
Believe me, than in half the creeds. [12]

We may now ask what it means to have faith in such a God as the last chapter has described. In general use, the word 'faith' has many shades of meaning. It is used to mean belief, knowledge, trust, hope, loyalty (as between marriage partners). Sometimes it seems to mean nothing more than gullibility, and some very astute thinkers have described it as wishful thinking, on which more later. Yet people of all religions and of none seem prepared to organise their whole lives on the basis of it. Christians regard faith, defined in various ways, as an important factor in their eternal salvation, and many non-religious people would say that faith in something is necessary if existence is to have meaning. So what is it? I should perhaps say at this point that I do not necessarily equate faith with religion, but for our purposes here I am concerned with the kind of faith which is expressed in religious – and specifically Christian – terms.

There are two distinct senses in which Christians use the word 'faith'. It may refer to 'the Faith', meaning some body of belief which exists in an objective way, independently of us, and it may also mean a more subjective response to 'the Faith' – our own personal commitment. I propose to look at the subject under both those headings. As in the last chapter, I shall attempt to face some hard issues; issues which I have certainly found disturbing, but which, far from destroying my own faith, have made it more meaningful and fulfilling. I cannot promise that the coming chapter will be comfortable reading, but I hope that in the end it will prove worth the risk.

[12] Alfred, Lord Tennyson: *In Memoriam A. H. H.* (1850) canto 96

I said earlier that I have found this to be the case. What I am trying to offer here is not a kind of vacuum-packed theology which is neatly presented, and must be accepted or rejected as it stands. Indeed, it is often easier to say what I do *not* believe than precisely what I do. My only qualification is that of a fellow traveller who cannot say what is at the end of the journey, but can say that the journey so far has proved worthwhile.

'The Faith'

For many people, there is something called 'the Faith', to which assent must be given if a person is to benefit from salvation. This is represented by a set of propositions about God, about scripture and – in Christian terms – about Jesus. The precise details range from the rather vague statement 'Jesus is Lord' of the early church to very complex systems of belief covering, in minute detail, everything from Creation to Judgment Day and what is thought to lie beyond. Further, the required *degree* of assent similarly varies. Does one need to believe, for example, in the six-day creation with the same conviction as one must have about the resurrection of Jesus? There have been many attempts to work out an 'irreducible minimum', or to put various doctrines into some kind of pecking order, but the flames of dispute have been fanned rather than extinguished, and not only the heretics have been burned. Since the 1980s when some old disputes re-emerged into the public arena, many have sought to include such doctrines as the virgin birth, the *physical* resurrection and the second coming of Christ in the 'irreducible minimum', and have claimed that debate should be closed on these matters. These things, it is said, are essential. They form part of the divine revelation; the foundation which cannot be disturbed without putting the entire structure of the faith at risk.

This model of the faith admittedly has a degree of certainty about it which many people find very comforting, but it poses immense problems, especially for those who are unable honestly to assent to what are presented as essential doctrines. We shall return to this point shortly, in considering personal faith.

More and more people are now openly questioning whether there is something so easily defined which we can call 'the Faith'; a set of eternal 'givens' handed down from time immemorial, which may not be questioned.

The quotation which opened this chapter points us to a different understanding of the concept of faith. Instead of simply accepting the handed-down ideas, we are invited to give our assent to a dynamic, growing understanding of God, the world and the relationship between the two. This understanding has been developing from the earliest days. It has been passed down by word of mouth, changing, growing and being refined in the process until (comparatively recently) it began to be written down in a systematised form. The process then continued, and what we now inherit is the still growing, still developing, still very much alive fruit of all that.

The Bible itself bears witness to this process and to the constant challenge to rethink established ideas. For example, the early Hebrews learned in the desert about the importance of cultic traditions, but later prophets, in different circumstances, had to tell them that there were other things which God valued more highly, as in the case of the prophet Amos whose utterances were devastatingly threatening to a people who had come to regard worship and ritual as the essentials of their religion.

> Even though you offer me your burnt offerings and grain offerings, I will not accept them; and the offerings of well-being of your fatted animals I will not look upon. Take away from me the noise of your songs; I will not listen to the melody of your harps. But let justice roll down like waters, and righteousness like an everflowing stream.[13]

[13] Amos 5:22-24

Traditional understandings of the nature of God and his relationship with people were radically challenged by, among others, Jeremiah who had to tell the people that their faith in the temple building was misplaced:

> Do not trust in these deceptive words: This is the temple of the Lord, the temple of the Lord, the temple of the Lord.'[14]

Throughout the Bible there are stories of characters who got into serious trouble for calling people to relinquish the apparent security of 'the Faith' and take the risk of moving on with God. The greatest of these, of course, is Jesus himself.

The most powerful argument for this dynamic concept lies in our understanding of the nature of God. The idea that there is a pre-packed commodity called 'the Faith', handed down from above, which must be accepted or rejected in its totality, is quite consistent with the *God in Control* model discussed in the previous chapter. But we have to ask whether the handing down of a take-it-or-leave-it package of beliefs, which we are not necessarily meant to understand but to accept unquestioningly, is the way a relational God would work. Would it not be quite inconsistent with his nature? God wants us freely to accept and reciprocate the love he offers. To say, 'This and this only is what you must think about me,' would be quite inconsistent. He wants us to grow: will he not seek to open our minds rather than close them? More to the point, can the whole truth about such a wondrous, mysterious, infinite God be neatly packaged and contained? Can the nature of the Infinite be adequately expressed in finite concepts and words? The very idea of the Infinite should tell us that we are going to have to think and speak in image and metaphor, rather than simple unambiguous statements. Images and metaphors have the advantage of being always open to further growth, under the

[14] Jeremiah 7:4

refining, developing influence of the Holy Spirit. Only by the use of this sort of language can a little of the mystery that is God be communicated to us, and only thus can our understanding grow. The insistence on narrow literalism is, in the end, a refusal to let God be God. To return to the analogy employed in the last chapter, we must ask whether in this most important matter of faith God is neurotically holding the string or whether he has had the confidence to let go. Has the toy been set free? Has it become 'real'? Creation can only be 'real' and not a toy, at the cost of some risk.

> 'Real isn't how you are made,' said the Skin Horse. 'It's a thing that happens to you. When a child loves you for a long, long time, not just to play with, but REALLY loves you, then you become Real.'
>
> 'Does it hurt?' asked the Rabbit.
>
> 'Sometimes,' said the Skin Horse, for he was always truthful. 'When you are Real, you don't mind being hurt.'
>
> 'Does it happen all at once, like being wound up,' he asked, 'or bit by bit?'
>
> 'It doesn't happen all at once,' said the Skin Horse. 'You become. It takes a long time. That's why it doesn't often happen to people who break easily, or have sharp edges, or have to be carefully kept. Generally, by the time you are Real, most of your hair has been loved off, and your eyes drop out, and you get loose in the joints and very shabby. But these things don't matter at all, because once you are Real you can't be ugly, except to people who don't understand.'[15]

[15] From *The Velveteen Rabbit* by Margery Williams

Clearly there has never been a static object called 'the Faith', handed down from generation to generation. Rather, as I have indicated, each successive generation was called to continue the journey of discovery, bringing its own set of insights and challenges and moving forward in new and often threatening directions; stepping out into the darkness. The faith was dynamic, growing, exciting and most of all *alive!*

This proposition of course does not merely imply that whatever was believed at any one stage of the process was incomplete and in some sense provisional; it calls us to recognise that our own conclusions and beliefs, however much better informed they might be, are also incomplete and provisional, and that applies also to whatever conclusions may be drawn from the present discussion. We are not called to accept what is handed down to us, but to participate in a process – a journey – learning from all that has gone before and at the same time looking eagerly forward to the discoveries ahead. In short, we are called to let God be God: the kind of God *he* chooses to be. And that means something rather greater than the insights of one particular period or tradition can even begin to express. The obvious questions this raises about the authority of scripture will be addressed in the next chapter. It suffices to say here that they are neither decisive nor insuperable.

This dynamic model of the faith offers us no certainty at all. It calls us to step into the darkness, and we have no way of knowing what is ahead of us. While we use the ideas and beliefs of the past as our starting point on the journey, there is no guarantee that we shall feel able to carry them with us. On the other hand, we might say that anything which is intended to give meaning to life *will* be dynamic rather than static, and anything dynamic involves risk and uncertainty. The problem then is whether risk and uncertainty are incompatible with faith. Perhaps there is a way out of the dilemma: perhaps it is possible to 'have faith' without having to have *a* faith; to be people of God without having to 'buy the package'. We shall see. Let us begin by looking at some of the popular traditional understandings of faith, and – lest it become threatening – let us remember that we do so as *people of faith.*

Personal Faith

If there is no pre-packed commodity we can call 'the Faith' then we have to ask what it means to be *people of faith.* I propose to do this by considering four words which are frequently used as synonyms for faith: knowledge, belief, trust and commitment. There are of course many more but the four I have chosen are fairly representative and include those others to a large extent.

Knowledge

Some great Christians of the past from various traditions have seen a close relationship between faith and knowledge. This has been variously expressed as 'faith *is* knowledge' and 'faith *leads* to knowledge'. Again, the desire for certainty is natural and powerful, and we can hardly blame anyone for seeking it. I well remember, after a crushing personal tragedy, claiming to myself and to others that I *knew* what in fact I desperately wanted – needed – to believe. However, as the grieving process went on I had to admit to myself that really I did not, and could not, *know* anything about life after death. Somehow I had to find a way of living without knowledge. Somehow I had to find *faith.* My wife and I have cause to be grateful to the friends who helped us to do that, at no little cost to themselves.

There have been many attempts over the centuries to prove the existence of God, but it is important to remember that the greatest thinkers recognised the limitations of that and did not seek to 'prove' God in the scientific sense. Rather, they sought to provide people of faith with some assurance that their faith was reasonable. An early example of this was produced by St Anselm, based upon the definition of God used in the last chapter: *That Than Which Nothing Greater Can Be Conceived.* Since it is greater to exist than not to exist,

God must be real. However, Anselm recognised the circularity of the argument which was, in any case, aimed at believers. Its purpose was really to say, 'Given that we believe in God, this is what he must be like.' As a scientific proof of the existence of God *per se*, it is clearly totally inadequate as, of course, Anselm himself knew.

Thomas Aquinas argued for a 'First Cause'. If we ask what propelled a snooker ball into the pocket, a simple answer is that it was struck by the cue ball. However, the real answer is that *somebody* first struck the cue ball. Similarly, Aquinas argued, the train of events connected with existence must have a First Cause, and it is this First Cause who gives meaning to the universe. This is tempting, but is easy to undermine. It depends on the idea that there is purpose in the universe, which there may be but there again there may not. The mere fact that we see *apparent* purpose and meaning in the universe does not mean that it is there. Humankind has had plenty of time to impose its own interpretations, but that does not mean that any of them are real.

The analogy of the watch, advanced by William Paley in the eighteenth century, is also tempting at first sight. It goes like this. If someone from a primitive culture discovered a watch lying on the ground, they could discern, without knowing what it was for, that it had both a designer and a purpose. Even if it were broken, the same deductions could be made. So, it is said, we can discern that the universe had a designer and a purpose, and the fact that it is apparently broken does not change that. Of course, we are still up against the assumption of design and purpose. How do we really know that the universe has design? What would be the chance of this intricate pattern of existence coming about by accident? It would probably be billions to one, but how do we know that there have not been billions of near misses before this happened? Come to that, it is theoretically possible for the outside chance to come about first time; ask any bookmaker who has had to pay out to a punter who successfully bet on an extreme outsider!

Even if we agree with the finder of the watch, and say there is design and purpose in the universe, that is all we are able to say. It does not say what the purpose is, or whether the designer is still around. He or she may be dead or may have conceded that the design has failed and gone off somewhere else to start again. Moreover, the *nature* of the designer is not clear. Many people see more reason to believe in a cynical God than a caring one. It is impossible to build a structure of religious belief, centred upon the presence of a loving God, on such 'evidence'.

There is much more that can be said on the subject of 'proofs' of God, but that is not necessary here. The point is that proof – and therefore knowledge *in the accepted sense* – is not to be had. Faith has much less to do with knowledge than it does with how we handle our uncertainty. However, while recognising the vital distinction between faith and knowledge, we must be careful not to oppose them as though they are incompatible. If we do that then we relegate faith to the realm of fantasy. We each have our own store of knowledge about the world and this plays a part in shaping our faith. We cannot *know* about God in the same way we can know about geometry, for example, but the knowledge we have can serve to point us in the direction of faith. Thus, having apparently dismissed the classical 'proofs of God', we may find a different kind of value in them.

> In common with many others, I have wished to revalue the classical 'proofs' of God's existence as suggestive insights rather than logically coercive demonstrations. They are part of those consilient 'converging lines of probable reasoning' which constitute a case for theism.[16]

In other words, we may not be able to prove the existence of God, but our knowledge of the way things work can provide us with a reasoned basis for faith.

[16] John Polkinghorne: *Science and Christian Belief* (SPCK 1994) p.41

Against those who seek to affirm that God can be proved beyond doubt by reasoned argument, Christian thinkers from St. Paul to Kierkegaard have recognised the limits of reason. The Christian call, according to them, is to commitment without certainty. The position then seems hopeless. God calls us to have faith in matters which reason cannot adequately prove, but also calls us to love him *with all our mind*, which seems to suggest that our reason should not be violated by our faith. What are we to make of that?

It is often said, with some justification, that the Roman Catholic tradition is authoritarian. People are called to accept what they are told and not to question it. In fact, this is a caricature. All caricatures have some basis in truth, and we must not ignore that, but they are not to be taken at face value. Certainly, the Catholic tradition has related faith to the assent to revealed truth. The acceptance of certain fundamental doctrines has always been seen as the basis of faith. However, the church has consistently claimed that such assent was 'reasonable': that while the articles of faith cannot be proved by reason they do not violate reason either. After all, it is necessary to begin somewhere, and the most rigorous scientific experiments begin with an assumption, which is then tested.

> While the search for truth requires a critical evaluation of the past (and present), it is not likely to be assisted by a negative scepticism. The risk of initial commitment to what appears to be the case is a necessary part of finding out what is actually the case. [17]

This is also the position of the churches: *fides quarens intellectum* – faith seeking understanding. We cannot *know*, but we can live in faith on the basis of reasonable belief. This is a long way away from the unquestioning credulity often

[17] John Polkinghorne: *Science and Christian Belief* (SPCK 1994) p.31

labelled 'faith'. It requires more than mere belief, calling for a high degree of commitment. And of course, the object of faith is ultimately God, and not the articles themselves.

While we are discussing the relationship between faith and knowledge, it is worth asking whether scientific proof of the existence of God would produce faith. On one level, at least, it would seem likely to make it redundant. More specifically – and more importantly – would knowledge result in faithful living? Elijah's experience on Mount Carmel[18] would seem to indicate the contrary. According to that story, the people had what in their times would have been regarded as proof positive of God, in a most spectacular form. We might suppose that such an experience as that would have 'put the fear of God into them' once and for all. But that does not seem to be the case, and Elijah's situation immediately afterwards made the victory seem a little hollow! It appears that even certain knowledge does not necessarily change people and make them faithful. We are more complex beings than that.

Belief

For many people, even if they do not see Christianity as a take-it-or-leave-it package, the word 'faith' must still mean 'belief'. They have identified their own irreducible minimum to which they subscribe. This actually applies to most of us, to one extent or another. Many, for example, regard the creation stories as myths or parables, but are absolutely committed to the gospel miracle stories as literal accounts of particular events. This kind of distinction is perfectly legitimate, saying as it does that there are many layers of meaning and many ways of expressing truth in scripture. It seems quite reasonable (especially in the light of science) to regard the six-day creation as symbolic while still holding that the miracles might literally have happened. It is also necessary to recognize that they represent different genres of writing, and thinking people will take that into account.

[18] 1 Kings 18:20-39

If faith is synonymous with belief, then it cannot be regarded as a virtue. Moreover, there is no way our personal salvation can be made to depend upon it in the way that is quite often preached. Later on I shall be arguing that faith involves the will, and the problem is precisely that belief does not. Let us take a non-religious example. I hope I may be forgiven for choosing what may seem like a frivolous one, but that may help to make the point.

In common, I suspect, with most readers of this book, I do not believe in fairies. That does not mean they do not exist. I could be wrong. I have never seen any and neither, as far as I know, has anyone whose opinions I regard as trustworthy, but that does not mean they are non-existent. The simple fact is that I am just not disposed to believe in them. I am not *free* to do so; my background, upbringing, temperament and perhaps much more conspire to make it impossible for me to believe. However wrong I might be, the simple fact is that I am freer not to believe than I am to believe. I can no more be held responsible for that than I can for the lack of atmosphere around the moon! In the same way, it is my firm conviction that there are people who, because of *their* background, upbringing, temperament or whatever, are not free to believe in God. Of course, I believe that God is working to set them free, and that is the vital distinction between this and the previous (inadequate) example. Yet history clearly shows that vast numbers of people depart this life in a condition of honest disbelief, despite (or perhaps because of) determined attempts to convince them. Are they to be punished for that? Are they to be described as faithless because they openly admitted to being unable to believe a certain set of propositions? It would appear from some of the traditional teachings about salvation that those who simply cannot believe in certain things with any integrity are in an impossible dilemma. Either they must be honest and face the dreadful consequences of unbelief, or they must be dishonest and make a futile attempt to convince an omniscient God that they believe in things which in their hearts they find untenable. Apparently they are, quite literally, 'damned if they do and damned if they don't'; they will go to hell either for disbelief or dishonesty! I remember a sermon in which a congregation was being exhorted to become engaged in evangelism. The preacher delivered what was clearly intended as a piece of brilliant rhetoric to show that sincerity in itself is not enough: 'People are going to hell for being sincerely wrong.' What this says about God of course is unthinkable. To compound the injustice, a significant number of those people have committed themselves to what many would see as Christlike sacrificial lifestyles; something generally more difficult for someone without the hope of eternal life which religious belief often includes. Is all that to be swept aside by a monstrous, pedantic God who cares more for what we *claim* to believe than for what we are? If faith is, as biblical tradition claims, essential for salvation, then either it is not simply to be equated with belief or God is a monster.

Trust

There is a significant element of trust in faith although, as we shall see, the two cannot be simply equated. However, once again we must acknowledge the dangers of simplistic thought. Eminent psychologists including Freud have described this kind of faith as wishful thinking. While this is undoubtedly too easy a generalisation, it has some truth in it. We need to be aware of the boundary between genuine faith and wishful thinking, although it is impossible to define with pinpoint accuracy.

When I applied for theological training, I spent a few days in the company of other hopefuls on a residential selection conference where one of the issues which was raised caused some very heated controversy. Most of us were 'mature students' with family commitments who had had plenty of time to become accustomed to having at least one, perhaps two secure incomes. Now we were contemplating uprooting our families and living on small student allowances paid by generous but struggling churches. So as a matter of pastoral concern as much as anything else, the college was anxious to ensure that we were not going to end up in desperate financial straits. Some candidates were clearly heavily committed financially, and would have difficulty, to say the least, in keeping solvent throughout the course. Some of those had thought it through and made provision, but one or two with even more substantial commitments could see no satisfactory answer and could only say, 'The Lord will provide.' The difficult question concerned whether that was said out of a deeply committed faith, or whether it was mere wishful thinking. Sometimes, what passes for faith is little different, if at all, from the sublime unworldly optimism of Mr. Micawber; an optimism for which others often paid.

It is a difficult question to know when faith becomes wishful thinking: how does one distinguish a burning faith from a blind obsession? One test, perhaps, is consistency. A real belief that 'The Lord will provide' should affect one's *whole* lifestyle, one's *every* decision; it cannot merely be used as a last resort on those occasions when our heart is trying to rule our head.

Of course the reader will object that I have caricatured trust. Perhaps, but really it is those who speak in that kind of way who do so. Trust is something quite different from wishful thinking, and I shall come to that shortly, but there is more to be said about the dangers of the latter. The trouble is that people frequently seem to think that if they say something often enough it will become true. Now this, of course, is not the view that seriously minded Christian people hold, and genuinely evangelical Christians would rightly object to being identified with this kind of nonsense, but it is a view which characterises the folk religion/superstition which has become common currency, and which sadly is to be found within the churches as well as outside. Most seriously, of course, *God in control* has now become *God under control* since we have learnt how to manipulate him.

Some people would validly say that faith and trust can only be genuine as part of a relationship, and this is what separates them from wishful thinking: we trust, or we have faith *in God*. This is absolutely true, but it does not dispense with the problems. If we say that faith works only if we are in a right relationship with God, then we are still in danger of over-simplification. It is an inconvenient fact that many people whose relationship with God seems to us to have been impeccable have suffered enormously – including Jesus himself. In our own century we only have to think of names such as Dietrich Bonhoeffer, Oscar Romero, Martin Luther King Jr., Jerzy Popieluzko, and the shallowness of wishful thinking becomes immediately apparent. Furthermore, the worst of it is, of course, that they did not suffer merely *in spite of* their relationship with God but precisely *because of it!* So the idea that those who do God's will are given some kind of special protection is clearly not tenable.

The answer often made to this point is that while they have undeniably suffered in this world they have their reward in heaven. Yet this argument really will not do, from people who are specifically claiming the rewards of 'faith' *in this world:* 'Trust in God and all will be well'! Neither will it do if we believe in a God who showed his commitment to *this* world by painfully immersing himself in it to the uttermost extent.

Here, then, is the essence of the distinction. Faith is not the same as trust, because trust has some empirical basis. We trust people on the strength of our experience of them. When someone has been a good friend for a long time we trust them to be there when they are needed. Trust is granted or withheld on the basis of experience. Yet Jesus, seeing his mission in tatters, his disciples scattered and his own life and reputation destroyed, is said to have died with a declaration of faith. Similarly, the twentieth-century martyrs to whom I referred above had all found that commitment to God brought anything but security. Their faith in a loving God was upheld in the face of monumental evidence to the contrary.

I am frequently told that it is wrong to argue in this way. If people's 'simple faith' gets them through life, and does no one else any harm, does it matter if it's naive? After all, it's not hurting anyone. It is, I am told, cruel and unnecessary to cause them to 'lose their faith'.

That is the point: genuine simple faith is to be encouraged, but what is described here is not simple but *simplistic* – and it *does* hurt people. What am I to say to the children of a woman who died of cancer in her early thirties, when they have effectively been told that if she or they had had enough faith, or prayed harder, or lived better, she would still be alive? What am I to say to the parents of a child who mysteriously died in his cot, and who blame themselves for it? What am I to say to the parents of a dead teenager who think that their honest and quite reasonable scepticism caused God to 'take him'? I have seen too many lives shattered in this kind of way, tried to reassemble too many broken personalities, to think that wishful thinking is harmless. It is harmful precisely because it is not true, and when it fails people are too frightened to blame God (and who can criticise them for that if he is so small-minded?) and so blame themselves instead, all too often with disastrous results for their own mental well-being. Wishful thinking is dangerous, and has no place in theology. Not only is it not harmless; it is deadly. It is the antithesis and the destroyer of faith, and the sooner it is lost the better.

Let us return to the idea of faith as trust. I have already said that the two cannot simply be equated, since trust normally is based on some degree of experience or knowledge, but there is clearly a link between the two. Perhaps we should ask how trust actually affects our actions. For example, would we say that we trusted someone's driving, but then refuse ever to be a passenger in the car with them? Would we say we trusted a baby-sitter, but ask a neighbour to pay frequent visits to check up? Here is the common ground between faith and trust. They both involve a degree of commitment, and a degree of risk. The claim to trust, or to have faith, is meaningless if we are not prepared to order our lives accordingly.

Commitment

> 'Tis not the dying for a faith that's so hard, Master Harry – every man of every nation has done that – 'tis the living up to it that is difficult.[19]

The last point has brought us to the heart of the matter. Faith is ultimately more than belief or knowledge, in that it involves the will. We cannot will ourselves to believe, but we can will ourselves to be faithful. A good example of that is marriage. Being faithful to my wife is not a matter of what I believe or know about her, but of how I relate to her. In the same way, being people of faith is much more about how we live in relation to our accepted beliefs than how firmly we believe them or whether they can be proved.

There is a fictional story about a man who was walking along a clifftop path when he slipped and fell over the edge. As luck would have it, he managed to grab a shrub growing out of the cliff face and check his fall, but he was then unable to move either up or down. Knowing that he would only be able to hang there for a limited length of time before his hands lost their grip, he racked his brains for a way of escape. He had never been a particularly religious type, but decided that in the absence of anything better he would give prayer a try. So, turning his eyes upward (to where he had always been told God was) he called out, 'Is there anyone up there who can help me?' Immediately, a bright light shone from the clouds and a voice replied, 'I can help you.' 'Who are you?' enquired the man. 'I'm God,' came the reply. With an enormous sense of relief, the man asked, 'What do you want me to do?' and received the astonishing answer: 'Let go of the shrub.' The man hung there for a few moments more before raising his eyes again and saying, in a faltering voice, 'Is there anyone else up there who can help me?'

[19] William Makepeace Thackeray: The History of Henry Esmond (1852) bk. 1, ch. 6

What was his problem? Were the light in the sky and the disembodied voice not adequate evidence? Perhaps we should ask ourselves whether we should have entrusted our lives to it, or whether we should rather have doubted our own sanity. After all, we are aware that there are significant numbers of people now in locked hospital wards and secure units who have heard voices telling them to do things which were dangerous to themselves or others. But that point, important though it is, is not the only one. Suppose our unfortunate friend fully accepts that this is the voice of God. What does he then know? He knows that some supernatural being exists, and is advising him to let go. That is all he knows, apart from the fact that he is hanging precariously over dangerous rocks. What he does not know is whether he can trust this God or not. He knows that God exists, but he does not *know God.* Perhaps the cynics have been right all along who have said that God exists but is not loving. Perhaps, on the contrary, he is a vindictive monster who regards creation as his plaything and delights in the pain of its inhabitants. We may be reasonably sure that our reluctant hero will determinedly seek other solutions before letting go of the shrub.

What he has to do is to make a life-commitment. But he has to do so without certainty. Perhaps if he holds onto the shrub for long enough he will be rescued. He does not know. Perhaps if he lets go God will keep his promise, but he does not know that, either. He will not know until after he has let go.

Of course, this story depends on the very model of God which I have rejected: *God in control.* It is quite obvious that I would not expect God actually to behave in this way, but nonetheless, the story is useful. The world is full of people – individuals and communities – who seem to be trapped between a static existence which is going nowhere and a great unknown which seems threatening. They do not like the shrub from which they are hanging, but they dare not risk the alternative. And the sad truth is that this is all too familiar a description of churches. Many churches are dying out in a vain attempt to preserve what little they have. In reality, they died years ago, when they took the decision to hang onto the shrub rather than let go in faith. It is a fundamental principle of the kingdom of God as Jesus saw it that we need to let go of what is most precious – even life itself – if we are to find what is of eternal significance.

> For those who want to save their life will lose it, and those who lose their life for my sake will find it.[20]

Cat's Cradle

In dividing up the argument into sections (necessarily, for the sake of clarity) I have of course oversimplified it, for while faith cannot simply be equated with knowledge, belief or trust it clearly must involve all of those to a greater or lesser degree. Otherwise, we are back to the wishful thinking phenomenon, and that is not at all healthy. Just as it is impossible to prove God, but very possible to put together an impressive body of circumstantial evidence which makes belief possible, so it is with a commitment of faith. There are some things which we know about the way things happen in the world which enable us to believe in a loving God. We can look at the powerful role of religious faith in history and be encouraged to hope that embracing that belief may not be futile and may indeed help make a difference to the world. Added to that is the testimony of scripture, which we shall consider in more detail shortly; and although I shall be arguing that it offers no guarantees, no crystal clear definitive proof, and indeed does not even speak with one unequivocal voice, yet we can discern within it strands and patterns which unify it, reinforce our inclination toward faith and make commitment more possible. Similarly in the traditions of the church and in individual Christian experience we may find much to make us

[20] Matthew 16:25

question, and even cause for cynicism; and yet it too contains threads which unite with the other elements to create a kind of supportive network – a 'cat's cradle' of criss-crossing strands – which can undergird our faith. None of these strands on its own would bear the weight, and the whole structure does not add up to an impenetrable argument; it will always be possible to find other ways of accounting for it. Yet for those who are inclined toward faith there is enough there to support it and enable it to grow.

So we might say that while faith cannot be easily defined and certainly cannot be crudely equated with belief or knowledge, those elements and many others are part of it. However, as I have already suggested, faith must be a dynamic which motivates, directs and enlivens us in the search not only for our own wholeness but that of all creation.

People of Faith

Faith is about how we live, in relation to our beliefs, much more than about what those beliefs are or how strongly we hold them. Kierkegaard encapsulated this point in a particularly cutting remark. Having described faith as 'floating on seventy thousand fathoms of water,' he observed, 'Mynster has never been out on seventy thousand fathoms in order to learn out there. He has always clung to the standard order of things and has now quite grown to it.'[21] This is a wonderfully evocative image. We shall not learn to swim without taking the risk of letting go. We have to be prepared to be out of our depth, so to speak.

I believe in God. I *know* that I am sitting in a chair and writing this on a word processor. I cannot claim to know anything about God in the same way as I know that.

I have faith in God. I do not have a great deal of faith in my word processor. That is why I keep back-up copies of everything I write. That is why I have a maintenance contract

[21] Journal (1847)

so that when the thing inevitably lets me down I can get it repaired. That is why I save my work to disk at regular intervals, so that if the machine goes up in smoke I shall still have most of the work. Because I do not have faith in my word processor, I take precautions, hedge my bets, cover my back.

I have faith in God. It is based on some ideas, teachings, concepts, which seem to me to be reasonable although I cannot prove them. They also seem to me (and this is really the point) to be significant for all creation. They say to me that there are things which it is worthwhile to live for and to die for: values which are of greater importance than my personal wealth or security. I believe those values come from God. I do not *know* that they do. I believe that they do, and although I cannot prove it my reason is not violated by that belief. None of that, though, actually makes me a person of faith. I will be a person of faith only as I order my life according to those beliefs. But there is no back-up system.

- I do not *know* there is a God
- If there is, I do not *know* he is as shown in Jesus
- I do not *know* that Christ is risen
- I do not *know* there is life after death.

That is not to say that I am without any kind of firm basis for faith, however, for I do have a body of accumulated knowledge which tends to point me in that kind of direction, or at least makes it not unreasonable to begin the journey. Most importantly, though, to be a person of faith, I do not need to *know* those things: I need to live by them. I must order my life according to the will and purpose of God so far as I understand them. It may at times be demanding, frightening, risky and costly. I shall sometimes be elated, sometimes frustrated and sometimes downright terrified, and in all that I can still be a person of faith if I commit myself utterly to that of which I cannot be certain.

I have sometimes been asked, 'What if you are wrong?' In other words, what if it turns out that God is the tyrant whom

I have rejected, and that I, with all my 'doubts' do not qualify for salvation? Ought I not to be doing all I can to secure my eternal future, by saying the right things and suppressing my questions? My only answer is that that would not be faith.

The unfortunate gentleman hanging off the cliff is finding out the hard way that faith means *letting go of certainty!* With regard to the existence of God, he has been granted the nearest thing to certainty that he will ever have in this world. And as we have seen, it's getting him nowhere. He has another kind of certainty: that as long as he holds onto the branch he won't fall to his death. The trouble is, he can't actually go anywhere, either. He's got to let go of the 'certainty'. He's got to take the risk. He may of course turn out to be wrong, but that's the decision he has got to make.

Of course, I can't be certain, but I think God actually wants my life to go somewhere. I'm going to live by that belief. I might be wrong, of course, and he might want me to spend my life dishonestly paying lip service to a lot of things which mean nothing to me, just for the sake of 'saving my soul'. For all the reasons above (and a good many more) I don't think so, but I can't be certain.

Faith provides the nearest thing I'm likely to get to an answer: let God be God. If God is truly God, then it does not depend upon me, but God cannot be God for me as long as I hedge my bets, and cling to illusory and short-term security.

Sin is the refusal to let God be God.

Faith, then, is letting God be God; on his terms and not mine.

That is why I've let go of the shrub.

CHAPTER THREE

SCRIPTURE AND THE WORD OF GOD

I expect most people know the story of the emperor's new clothes. A pair of rogues flattered the emperor into paying a large sum of money for non-existent clothes. It needed, they said, an intelligent person to appreciate them; fools could not see the new suit. The result was that the emperor went out in public quite naked, the crowd having been well primed in advance. Everyone, not wanting to appear a fool, acclaimed the new clothes; everyone, that is, except a small boy who somehow had missed the publicity and did not know the secret. So he gleefully proclaimed to all and sundry that the emperor was naked. What a pity he did not know what he was supposed to think!

So, a question: who served the emperor best: those who unquestioningly swallowed the official line, or the one who, for whatever reason, saw and recognised the reality? Until – in historical terms – comparatively recently, Christians were generally sold an official line about something which is of fundamental importance to our faith: the nature of scripture. Those who questioned the official line were met with the same kind of incredulity as if they had dared to point out that the emperor had no clothes, but their fate was immeasurably worse. Fortunately this is much less prevalent now than it once was, and many who gladly accept the theological label 'conservative' are open to (and indeed engaged in) critical study of the scripture texts. However, one can also discern a reaction against this which gives rise to a worrying kind of neo-fundamentalism.

Since the way we understand scripture, and what we understand it to be, is a vital part of the foundations upon which our faith rests, we shall have to pay due attention to it.

Could it be that this is another candidate for excavation and reinforcement?[22] Are we going to have to dig away, carefully, at the way of understanding scripture which has been so important to us and replace it (the understanding, not the scripture) with something else? It would be appropriate here to say a few words about the range of approaches to scripture.

The popular caricature in which the world of theology is divided into two groups conveniently but simplistically labelled 'conservatives' and 'liberals' does not do justice to the reality. Those who subscribe to it tend to classify 'conservatives' as those who continue to believe that the emperor has beautiful clothes (and dare not think otherwise for without them he could not be the emperor) and 'liberals' as those others who disdainfully point out that he is naked and then also go on to say that therefore he is not the emperor. In reality, of course, this is a gross oversimplification. Certainly both of those groups exist, but there are many others in between them. As well as the many 'conservatives' I have mentioned who engage in critical appraisal of scripture, there are also 'liberals' who wish not to discard the Bible but to rediscover its true significance. Also, it must be said, there are those who, from a supposedly 'liberal' perspective, reject biblical authority every bit as uncritically as the most ardent fundamentalist clings to it. Whilst at theological college I shared the course and a regular train journey with a student who happily labelled himself a fundamentalist. From an initial relationship of reciprocated distrust we gradually developed a firm friendship and mutual respect as each found that the other did not fit the usual stereotypes. He learnt that one can be a liberal and still be committed to the Bible; I learnt that 'fundamentalist' does not need to mean 'narrow minded'. In what follows, it would be easy to feed the false stereotypes, and the reader, as well as the author, must bear that danger in mind.

[22] cf. chapter 1

The fundamental basis of the claim about the emperor's new clothes was that the emperor himself appeared convinced about them. And who will argue with the emperor? We who place ourselves under the authority of scripture find that it *apparently* claims to be infallible. And who will argue with scripture? If this appears to be trivialising the issue I make no apology. The very absurdity of the analogy makes the point. Scripture cannot be held to be infallible merely by its own claim. To accept that claim unthinkingly and then to submit unquestioningly to the authority which we have thereby conferred is to fail to take the book seriously. If it really were infallible, then it should fear no challenge.

Comparatively recent developments in theology have exposed the Bible to critical scrutiny. Far from being presumptuous, as is sometimes claimed, this is a mark of respect. To protect the Bible from critical scrutiny would be to patronise it, as may be illustrated by an example from the world of music. When Tschaikovsky sent the score of his *Voyevoda Dances* to Balakirev, at the latter's request, he asked for a word of encouragement. This was understandable as he had recently been severely criticised. Balakirev's eventual reply was that encouragement was for children, whereas Tschaikovsky was 'a mature artist worthy of severe criticism.'[23] If scripture deserves to be taken seriously at all, and especially if it were ever to live up to the claim of infallibility, then it must be open to the most rigorous critical appraisal.

THE VOICE OF REASON

Obviously, the claim that scripture is infallible must be tested against more objective criteria than its own claims. In view of the previous chapter, we must ask not whether it can be proved by reason but whether it violates reason. On this test it immediately becomes obvious that scripture is not infallible.

[23] Edwin Evans: *Tschaikovsky* (Dent, 1966) p.25

Simple examples come readily to mind, such as the two quite distinctive accounts of creation. Despite many and ingenious attempts to harmonise them, they simply are irreconcilable as literal accounts. In the first, the whole of creation including animal and marine life is completed before human beings are made; but in the second, Adam and Eve are created *before* the animals. Now this may seem to be pedantic, but it is surely the kind of mistake which God would hardly be expected to make. Less pedantic, perhaps, being of more immediate concern, is the matter of the resurrection. Did the women clutch Jesus' feet, or did they run away in terror? Did they tell everyone but were not believed, or did they 'say nothing to anyone because they were afraid'? These are but a few examples among many. Those who wish to claim literal historicity for the Bible must confront these issues, and countless others like them. For those who do not make that claim, however, these differences reveal exciting depths of meaning in this multi-layered book we call scripture. More on that shortly.

The really puzzling thing about the claim to infallibility concerns translations. Assuming that the original documents were dictated, it seems odd that God then allowed fallible translators to make mistakes. The abundance of distinctly different translations of the Bible in our own time is in itself a stumbling block, but it is nothing new. Even within the Bible itself there are problems brought about by different translations. As with 'the Faith', discussed in the previous chapter, so with the Bible, there is no one single, definitive article. Even in the time of Christ, various translations abounded *and they did not agree.* This seems to make the original exercise of dictating an infallible text rather pointless. Had the original text in fact been infallible, surely God would have taken the elementary step of ensuring that the translations were faithful to it. After all, an infallible text is of little use if it is fallibly translated, especially when the infallible originals are then lost!

Even Rabbis, before the time of Christ, recognised that there was a problem; they did not accept the Bible as literal.

The solution they offer to the problem is to say that God did indeed inspire the Bible, but never meant it to be taken literally. Those elements which cannot be accepted as literal are described as allegory, parable and the like. But even then, there is still a problem. Not all the difficult passages can be so easily rationalised, for the fundamental issue is less the credibility of the stories as such than the nature of the God whom they portray. In the Old Testament, and indeed in some parts of the New, God appears to be contemplating acts of revenge against his enemies which make it difficult to recognise him as the God of Jesus. I have observed before that God is not generally considered to be a hypocrite, in which case we cannot let him off the hook by saying that it's all right if God does it but not if we do. The God who, in Jesus, called us to forgive until we have lost count (i.e. infinitely) cannot behave differently himself. And of course we do not need to look to the New Testament to find this contradiction; it is patently obvious in the Old Testament that different understandings of God were vying for supremacy. The stories which grew up around the person of King David illustrate this very well. Take for example the story about David's abortive attempt to bring the Ark of the Covenant to Jerusalem[24]. We are asked to believe that Uzzah was killed by God as punishment for touching the Ark with the perfectly reasonable intention of saving it from harm. This petulant action by God had the effect of delaying the whole enterprise one month, and changing the basis of his relationship with David from love and joy to anger and fear. We would be right, of course, in saying that this is hardly the God and Father of Jesus Christ, but we do not need to look so far away for a contrast. Very much within the Old Testament, Hosea wants us to believe in a God of infinite suffering love; using imagery appropriate to his day, he portrays God as akin to the wounded husband of an unfaithful wife who wears his heart on his sleeve and seeks to heal rather than to retaliate.

[24] 1 Chronicles 13

There are countless other examples which could be cited. What sort of a God kills the baby of an adulterous murderer (for such was the acclaimed writer of Psalm 23) in order to punish the parent? I have no difficulty believing that such an event in such circumstances would in those days have been regarded as God's judgment (a concept we shall consider in a separate chapter), but that is no excuse for us to perpetuate the slander against God, when we have reason to know better. We might also question the apparent sanctifying of David's bloodthirstiness; the basis of his popularity and the sign of his divine calling apparently was that he had killed ten times as many people as his predecessor. There, apparently, is the dilemma we face: either God was like that then, which poses insuperable problems for us now, or the biblical writers got it wrong.

That, of course, is a gross oversimplification since scholars will rightly argue that there are other ways of understanding passages of this kind. However, that does not invalidate the questioning; rather, it reinforces it since in saying that we concede that the stories cannot simply be accepted at face value.

Many voices, many accents

One of the problems with too simplistic a view of scripture whether from a 'conservative' or 'liberal' stance, is that it fails to take into account the different genres of writing. In reality the Bible is not so much a book as a library. Like any good library, it has gathered together writings from a wide variety of times and sources. Some of the writings may be described – in the best sense of the word – as *myth;* that is, they are not strictly factual but have been specifically written in order to convey truths, ideas, teachings, or simply to encourage us to think through the questions they have raised. Some of the books in the library are primarily collections of poetry or songs; others are historical records; some (such as Proverbs) are wisdom literature; some are legal text books exploring the intricacies of the Hebrew Law. A very important genre is *apocalyptic* literature, such as Daniel and Revelation. These writings are not the work of clairvoyants but of visionaries. They present God's future in dramatic images. Much of it is also subversive writing, intended to convey the hope of liberation to oppressed people in terms which they would understand but their oppressors (from a different cultural perspective) would not, hence some very mysterious and frightening images.

The variety does not end there. Many books cannot simply be slotted into one or other category since the writers (like modern authors) drew on a variety of sources and expressed themselves in metaphor, in parable and in pictorial images. Furthermore of course we cannot even simply ascribe an author to each book. We can often see evidence of the work of many authors, sometimes over long periods of time, being brought together into one volume.

This variety is not of course a weakness but a strength, in that it reveals a range of different emphases in the stories, which speak to us in fresh and exciting ways. Attempts to harmonise the apparent contradictions simply impoverish the Bible. One example of this can readily be found by comparing the gospel accounts. Putting it very simply, the first three, generally known as the synoptics, are basically in narrative form and attempt to give a *synopsis* of the life and work of Jesus while the fourth, the Gospel According to John, is much more of a theological statement. Clearly, this distinction cannot be hard and fast, since there is abundant theology in the synoptics and a good deal of narrative in John, but as a general classification it is fairly adequate. A concrete example of the effect of this can be found in the accounts of the passion of Christ. While all the writers make an association between the Passover feast and the crucifixion, John goes much further in having Jesus die at the precise moment the sacrificial lambs are being slaughtered in the temple, and thus he brilliantly highlights an image which he presented to us very early in the gospel.

> The next day [John] saw Jesus coming toward him and declared, 'Here is the Lamb of God who takes away the sin of the world!'[25]

All of this means that we should not expect the Bible to read like a kind of instruction manual for how to live our lives. We have to take into account not only the writers themselves but their times and circumstances, the influences of cultures other than their own and most of all the various images of God which they had in their minds.

The Bible as History

Only a few years before writing this book, I should have been most reluctant to describe the Bible in this way, but then I never was any good at history . . .

Like many children whose education began in or before the early fifties, I grew up with the illusion that history was the recording and learning of indisputable facts about the past. It never occurred to me to question either the literal accuracy or the apparent irrelevance of the subject. Perhaps we need to recover the French word histoire which covers both history and story. Fact and fiction are not the total opposites we take them to be, and a tender reconciliation is well overdue! So one of the first tasks of the tutors who, much later, bravely undertook my theological education was to open my mind to a subject on which it was firmly closed. I am indebted to the church historian Dr Barrie White who actually managed to arouse my curiosity enough to unlock the door.

The dry 'facts' which I mistook for the finished product of history are in fact merely a small part of the resources which it uses. It is impossible to write history without interpreting it, which means that almost every 'historical fact' must be constantly open to re-examination and revision. It is well said that history tends to be written by the winners, not the losers. In 1992 we were urged to celebrate the five hundredth

[25] John 1:29

anniversary of Christopher Columbus's 'discovery' of the 'New World' (and now I have used two clichés which the dispossessed of Latin America rightly find offensive!). The history written by the 'winners' justified that celebration: after all, the colonising countries had not only benefited themselves but had spread 'Christian Civilisation'. However, the 'losers' are now telling their history, and it is one of colonisation, of exploitation, of brutality, of religious and cultural imperialism and of the continuation of that in the present by a combination of military and economic muscle. So history is revealed to be far from a record of indisputable fact while yet being vital, powerful and highly relevant to the modern day. For all those reasons, I am happy to call the Bible history.

The Bible contains much that can be regarded as historical data. However, we can also see how the historians' perspective is affected by whether they were on the winning or the losing side of history. The Bible, therefore, is (from that point of view) to be read with as much caution as any other history book. However, there is more to it than that.

> The Bible *tells a story*. Human beings began to write history, say some historians, with the Bible. Biblical faith means knowing history and believing in the God who reveals himself in it.[26]

The Bible is the history of the slow and tortuous development of the relationship between God and a particular part of creation. As such it has all the relevance of any historical record. There is much that we can learn from the events it records (sometimes with frightening honesty) and also from the way in which they are recorded. The Hebrew historians understood the importance of history much better than I (or I suspect my school history teacher) did. They knew that the most important thing for a historian to do is to convey the

[26] Gustavo Gutierrez: *The Power of the Poor in History* (SCM 1983) p.5

meaning of history. They also knew (most of them, anyway) that lists of facts and figures were unlikely to hold the reader's interest for very long. So they told stories which at once made the statistics easier to hear and also brought out the meaning. They wanted to show not only what happens when people get on well with God, but what happens when they do not. They wanted to show humanity at its best and most hopeful as well as at its worst and most despairing. Most of all, they wanted to show the presence and activity of God in all that history.

We may safely accept, therefore, that some of the record may well be historically accurate and unembellished, some is likely to have been written by people who had an axe to grind, and some has certainly been dressed up in colourful ways in order to convey its essential meaning all the better. In accepting all that, we are opening ourselves to the God who lives in and speaks through all history, and that means that we take the Bible, as history, with utter seriousness.

Divine Inspiration

It may seem logical to proceed from where we are now to the conclusion that scripture cannot be divinely inspired. If it were it would be infallible. However, to make that link in simple terms would be to give credence to the *God in control* model which I have already rejected. In effect, we should be saying, 'If God had inspired the writers, they could not have got anything wrong.' I do not think that is a necessary progression of thought. At the same time, though, if we are to be true to the relational model, we may have to rethink our understanding of inspiration.

Inspired Art

An artist may be said to be 'inspired'. That does not mean she is going to reproduce, on canvas, in words or music, exactly what had inspired her. The paintings of Picasso or the French impressionists, for example, can certainly claim to be inspired by someone or something, but do not portray that source exactly. There is little point in having an artist if what is required is a facsimile. Artists, in all spheres of art, bring their own gifts, perceptions, emotions to bear upon their work. Even a photographer does not produce a mere replica of the subject but arranges lighting, chooses lenses and filters, to *interpret* what the eye sees. So the same subject can be portrayed in many ways, all of them valid. A painter may look at Yorkshire's Swaledale landscape and see principally the beauty of the colours and contours, highlighted by sun and cloud. Another may see the hostility which the environment can represent to, for example, a stranded walker. A third may see the rugged grandeur as a symbol of all that is best in creation, while a fourth feels drawn to express praise to God. When I visited an artist's studio in the Yorkshire Dales, I was struck by the rather unreal, dreamlike quality of the work. Later, in conversation, the artist told me that he had no concern with the world beyond his village. International affairs were of no interest to him; he merely wanted to shut himself away and paint. The fact that this was the time of the cold war and he lived a few miles from Catterick military base made me wonder whether he had chosen the best place for his reclusive life. But the point is that his own personality, priorities and attitudes had influenced his work. His view of the Dales as a kind of Garden of Eden in which he could hide was well represented by his style.

So if we say that scripture is inspired it does not necessarily have to mean that it is infallible. The question is, *how* does God inspire? According to the relational understanding to which I am committed, God allows the personality of the writer full scope. What the biblical writer is giving us is an insight into his or her relationship with God and the understanding both of God and the world which that relationship creates. This relationship is coloured by many influences, and these come through. The stories of David, for example, show a conviction that God is faithful and just; that he demands high ethical standards; that wrongdoing must have its consequences, and much more besides, all of which is valuable and healthy. Unfortunately, God's respect for the inspired writer's freedom means that some of these ideas are expressed in ways which a more enlightened readership might find offensive, but that does not invalidate the basic points. However, if we are to sift out the healthy from the unhealthy then we must do so freely, without the constraints of a narrow understanding of inspiration. The vital factor in this process is not the 'infallibility' of scripture but the nature of God.

The Uniqueness of Scripture

From the idea of the inspiration of scripture there traditionally follows the claim that it is unique. This is an easier concept to accept if we do not confuse uniqueness with exclusiveness. The Bible is certainly unique. Developed first in an oral tradition and then written down over many centuries, by writers from a wide geographical, social and theological spectrum, it records as no other book the tortuous, growing relationship between a particular group of people and God. It show us the highs and lows, the celebrations and the tragedies of that relationship and it offers images which are rich in significance for all generations. It is the foundational book for any knowledge of the God of Judaism and Christianity, and any attempt at Christian theology which did not take the Bible seriously would be futile.

What all that does *not* mean is that the Bible says all there is to say about God and the world. We must surely believe that God has not stopped speaking, that our relationship with him has not stopped growing, and that the infinite creative possibilities of God have not been exhausted. Most importantly, God has not been ultimately defined and described. Is it not possible he is inspiring writers, poets, painters, musicians, orators, thinkers and indeed anyone who is open to the inspiration?

J. R. R. Tolkien's book, *The Hobbit* is about a fairly insignificant character who finds himself caught up in cataclysmic events, and only then discovers his real potential. In the course of his adventures, the evil dragon, Smaug, who has plundered and terrorised the known world, is killed. We might expect this to be the end of the story, but it is far from that. Before the celebrations have died down, the newly liberated inhabitants of the world are squabbling over the dividing up of Smaug's treasure instead of enjoying the peace and liberty they could now have. Ancient rivalries, readily forgotten in the fight against the common oppressor, now threaten to destroy all the benefits of liberation.

Anyone reading this book, or reflecting upon it, during the break-up of the Soviet Union, might have seen it as a timely warning, a prophecy even, of what has since unhappily taken place. Not that one needs to be a student of political history in order to enjoy the book on other than a superficial level. It is peppered with apparently simple phrases and sentences which turn out to have many facets and layers of meaning.

> The Bagginses [were considered] very respectable, not only because they were very rich, but also because they never had any adventures or did anything unexpected.[27]

Bilbo Baggins is called upon to have an adventure, which means that he risks losing his neighbours' respect by doing something adventurous. The reader is invited to judge whether he gained anything else in place of it. Would it be too much to say that Tolkien was divinely inspired?

After the humiliation of a beaten enemy following the first world war, in which the seeds of the second were liberally sown, John Drinkwater wanted to show a better way of dealing with a defeated enemy. He could have written to the papers or mounted a soap box to speak on the subject; he could even, perhaps, have tried to secure a slot on radio. He chose to write a play. He called it *Abraham Lincoln* and in it

[27] J. R. R. Tolkien: *The Hobbit* chapter 1

he dramatised the political background to the American civil war. The audience, seeing the way the surrender of the Confederate army was received, were tacitly invited to reflect on the proper way to treat a defeated enemy. Drinkwater had presented his message in a way which made it easier for his audience to hear and accept. What an inspired idea! Not being a historian, I cannot comment on the strict accuracy of the storyline, but I should be surprised if it had not been freely shaped in order to make the point Drinkwater wanted to make.

It will be objected that all those things could be found in the Bible, without recourse to more recent literature. This may be true, but the point is that familiarity has dulled our understanding. The great works of art can send us back to our Bibles with newly opened eyes, to appreciate things which we might never have recognised in over-familiar texts now heavily overlaid with traditional, orthodox interpretations. However, I should want to go further. Presumably, the infinite God has new truths to reveal; truths which will certainly be consistent with what is found in the Bible, but which may well take us beyond it, opening up exciting new insights into God and his creative possibility.

These examples of course raise another issue. Purists will object that neither Tolkien nor Drinkwater was aware of divine inspiration. They did not set out to write religious truths. It may further be claimed, quite legitimately, that Tolkien was not trying to change the world, but to write an exciting adventure story for children. I have no problem with either point; they are both valid, although I should be surprised if anyone who wrote for children (except for purely pecuniary reasons) was not hoping to teach them something at the same time. The best children's books have many layers of meaning. *Alice in Wonderland; Winnie the Pooh; The Chronicles of Narnia;* all those are good examples of the point.

Apart from that, *we have to let God be God!* He is not to be restricted to speaking only through certain people or certain media. He is everywhere; there is no part of creation from which he is absent. Quite correctly, Christians are very ready to give God the credit for anything good, in which case it is only logical to assume that he has played a part in the production of the best art, literature, music etc. He is able to speak to us through any part of his creation, and if an artist, an author or an architect is open to truth then God will help them to express it, whatever their particular religious convictions.

All this is not to undermine the uniqueness of scripture; rather, I simply want to point out that it is not the *only* literature through which God speaks. Certainly it is the book through which we most readily expect to hear him, but there can be no doubt that he is inspiring creative writers today, and we should not cut ourselves off from what he is saying to us there.

Let God be God. Let him be free to speak to us (that is, let us make ourselves open to hear) through any media of *his* choosing, from the *Daily Mirror* to *War and Peace,* and supremely, although not exclusively, through the Bible.

THE WORD OF GOD

What do we now make of the traditional claim that scripture is 'the word of God'? In the Bible the 'word of the Lord' is singular and particular. The traditional claim of the prophets was, 'This is the word of the Lord,' rather than 'These are the words of the Lord.' The word is personal, as indicated by the frequent use of the phrase, 'The word of the Lord came to . . .' So it has been said that the 'word of the Lord' is the person of God speaking. It does not refer to some message handed down in oral or written form, but to the actual presence of God, speaking to us. That presence may be mediated through a person or a book, or perhaps these days through a video film or computer disk, but it is not to be simplistically *identified* with any of those. The word of God is received in relationship; it is not a static commodity which can be packaged, bought and sold. The word of God is personal and relational.

So it would be more accurate to say that the Bible is the primary *witness* to the word of God. Not only is this term more accurate; it is less open to idolatry. The Bible is not God. It has no miraculous powers of its own. Yet all too often we find the living God replaced by one of paper and ink. This is not confined to heretical sects. In many mainstream churches we can see this valuable book put on a pedestal (not necesssarily the same thing at all as a lectern!) and, in effect, worshipped. Obviously, pointing this out invites a scornful response, but it takes little effort to discern the idolatry.

At my ordination I was presented with a Bible. I value it for what it represents, but I do not worship it. Shortly after I had it, I found that the leather cover was curling because it had been left on a windowsill, and in order to prevent further damage I placed another heavy book on top, to flatten it again. A friend commented that her mother, who was undoubtedly a good, devout Christian and no idolater, would have been horrified to see something else placed on top of the Bible. And these reservations are deep-seated. Not long ago, my wife and I had to accommodate to a smaller house and a smaller study. It was time to be ruthless; a lot of things would have to go. Looking through my books, I found quite a number which were clearly not worth keeping, and happily put them aside to be disposed of. However, I then came upon a few very old, very battered Bibles which simply duplicated what was on my shelves – already groaning under the weight of most of the modern translations available. Why did I then feel an odd qualm about disposing of them? I have plenty of Bibles; like all ministers, I probably have more than the great majority of Bible-loving Christians. Like the other books in the box, they were surplus to requirements. More than that, their age and condition meant they were not much use to anyone else, either. I disposed of them, but what is significant here is the considerable unease with which I did so; an unease born of a traditional reverence for the book itself which has obviously sunk deeper into my being than I like to admit.

Bibliolatry is, of course, a national trait. Why, we may ask, do we still ask people to swear on the Bible (a doubtful practice itself, from a scriptural point of view) before giving evidence in a court of law ? The value in terms of securing the truth is immensely doubtful. This is of course a hangover from the days when the book itself (which most people could not read for themselves even if they possessed one) was the object of superstition. Now that one can walk into W. H. Smith and buy one, perhaps a few shelves lower than the pornography and fairly close to the mythology section, and most people are capable of reading it for themselves, that mystique has, thankfully, considerably declined. Unfortunately, it hangs on in the very place where it should not: the churches. I remember a conversation I had with the pastor of a church heavily involved in 'deliverance ministry'. He told me of a technique he used with people who were thought to be 'possessed', which involved touching them with a Bible. He claimed that people had literally recoiled as though it were hot. 'That,' he said smugly, 'is the power of the *Word of God*,' unconsciously and significantly dropping into a transatlantic drawl as he pronounced the last three words! I do not doubt that people had certainly recoiled as he touched them. Having first been thoroughly filled up with all of that nonsense, I am sure that I should have done so too. The people he worked with were certainly possessed, but by what is another matter.

That is an extreme example, but in different forms and different degrees of intensity, bibliolatry is to be found all around us, and it is the most sure-fire way of seeing that the Bible is not taken seriously. Perhaps I should offer some illustration of that point.

I once bought a postcard which had on it a picture of a disabled woman in a wheelchair. The odd thing was that she was on a pedestal several feet off the ground. Round the bottom of the pedestal, people were bowing, laying flowers and saying, 'We think you're wonderful!' The card was a protest against that romanticising of disability which clearly reveals that disabled people are not taken seriously. As long as she was on that pedestal, the woman could do nothing. She had no contribution to make to society. From the point of view of her unwelcome worshippers, of course, she was safely out of the way where she could not challenge them, could not even communicate with them, but they were able to pretend to be committed to her.

I saw that same thing done to the Bible at a service in a church belonging to a mainstream denomination. The preacher had been specifically invited for Bible Sunday, and evidently regarded it as his job to ensure that we all felt a suitable degree of awe for the Bible. He stood in the pulpit and waved it in the air. He riffled the pages. He smelt the soft leather cover. And he told us that it said things which it simply does not. The only thing he never did was read from it.

That is why we should never put the Bible on a pedestal and worship it.

Taking Scripture Seriously

Now I find myself actually taking scripture seriously. Having stated my conviction that the emperor has no clothes, I can embark on an honest – if somewhat disturbing – dialogue. And then it is that I make a startling discovery. This naked potentate is in fact a person of amazing depths, whom I want to get to know more and more. The Bible is actually attractive, stimulating, inspiring, now that the pretence is dropped and I can relate honestly to it. As long as I was trying to pretend it was something which, in my heart of hearts, I knew it was not, this was impossible. The emperor has not changed. I have. I have made the amazing discovery that nakedness is OK! All my life, I have wanted to believe the emperor had fine clothes, *because everybody told me he could not be the emperor without them!* That was not the case. The emperor could be the emperor without his clothes; it was the world which had the problem in accepting him without them. So it pretended to have dressed him up in finery which made him acceptable, made him conform to its ideas of imperial authority and then, when faced with the naked truth, simply denied it.

The Bible is a fascinating, wonderful book through which God can and does speak to us. This is not completely hidden if it is dressed up in claims of infallibility, but those claims become a distraction. Instead of listening to it, we spend our time and energy defending it. The time and resources devoted to convincing the people that the emperor had fine clothes would have been much better used in winning the hearts and minds of the people to what he stood for. We have failed to do the latter because we have been too busy doing the former.

The Law and the Prophets

The Law

On the basis of what has gone before, we can say that the Law, as set out in the Ten Commandments, was divinely inspired without then having to say that it is unchangeable or infallible. This seems like dangerous ground indeed; for many this is the very foundation upon which civilised existence rests. If we are to dig underneath it, what is to prevent the whole edifice which it supports from collapsing in the kind of way I had expected my church building to do?

That, of course, was precisely the pharisees' objection to Jesus. Between Moses and them lay a long tradition of interpretation of the law. The Ten Commandments had been found to be a little vague, and had needed elaboration from the lawyers. Let us take an example which Jesus found particularly thorny: Sabbath observance.

The Ten Commandments made it clear. There was to be no work on the Sabbath. No one was excluded from that; it applied to everyone, even the visitors. It does not take much imagination to realise that it soon became unworkable. To begin with, what about priests? They had their job to do and, although they did not work a one-day week any more than present day clergy do, their most obvious working day was precisely the one they were supposed to take as a rest day.

Furthermore, the current heresy of individualism had not at that time caught on, and the value of a *communal* quiet day was recognised. So it was not a simple matter of taking a different day. Special dispensation had to be given to the priests, and God's apparent oversight was corrected, or one of them was. Within a week of the law being enacted, of course, they would realise another problem. Animals might not be working but they still need to be cared for, and they can also get into trouble. So came another amendment, which later enabled Jesus to point out that animals were valued more highly on the Sabbath than were people![28] Then, of course, the very word 'work' required definition. Was walking work? People had to get to the place of worship somehow. So we find in the Bible the term 'a Sabbath day's journey', referring to the specific distance which the rabbis had decreed could be walked without breaking the law. Thus we can see, even within this most sacred tradition, an openness to change and recognition of the provisional nature of the law.

Jesus clearly thought that the basic commandments were 'inspired' in some sense, but was quite scathing about the way the law was used. He did not shrink from bringing the qualities of common sense and compassion to bear upon the law.

This is not to say that Jesus was a simple libertarian. He was no anarchist. In the passage from the Sermon on the Mount known as the Antitheses, he indicates that, far from being too strict, the law is not demanding enough in some areas. He calls his followers to go beyond it. Jesus is not setting the law aside but extending it.

> Do not think that I have come to abolish the law or the prophets; I have come not to abolish but to fulfil. For truly I tell you, until heaven and earth pass away, not one letter, not one stroke of a letter, will pass from the

[28] Luke 13:15-16

> law until all is accomplished. Therefore, whoever breaks one of the least of these commandments, and teaches others to do the same, will be called least in the kingdom of heaven; but whoever does them and teaches them will be called great in the kingdom of heaven. For I tell you, *unless your righteousness exceeds that of the scribes and Pharisees,* you will never enter the kingdom of heaven.[29]

Jesus thought it quite legitimate to update the Bible. In the famous answer to the question of divorce, for example, he made it clear that the law had been made *for the circumstances of the time.* Now it may be objected that it is one thing for Jesus to modify the law, but not for us. Even if that argument were accepted, we should still be faced with the fact that Jesus himself clearly believed that the law was provisional – written for that particular set of circumstances:

> They said to him, 'Why then did Moses command us to give a certificate of dismissal and to divorce her?' He said to them, 'It was because you were so hard-hearted that Moses allowed you to divorce your wives, but from the beginning it was not so. And I say to you, whoever divorces his wife, except for unchastity, and marries another commits adultery.'[30]

We should bear a cautionary point in mind. The fact that Jesus recognises the provisional nature of this law does not mean that it is entirely invalidated. As I have already observed, Jesus actually goes on to strengthen it in many

[29] Mat 5:17-20 (My Italics)
[30] Mat 19:7-9

cases. Even where he does not, he seeks to restore the true value of it, rather than dismiss it. We are reminded that the law is there for the benefit of people, and not to enslave them. So when we say that the Bible is provisional, we do not imply that it can be treated in a cavalier fashion. On the contrary, we have even more responsibility to see that it is taken seriously.

The Prophets

Surely, here is evidence for the literal inspiration of scripture, as well as for the *God in control* model and all that goes with it? How can we possibly explain the presence in scripture of so many prophecies which came true, if it is not a very direct revelation from God?

The first objection to that is the same as to all the other 'proofs'. It simply does not prove anything. If we are going to apply that criterion to scripture, then we must apply it elsewhere. On the basis of that reasoning, some would say that the writings of Nostradamus should be given equal status with the Bible, a contention which would be fiercely and correctly disputed. There may be many reasons why prophecies come true, which have nothing to do with religion, as such. We cannot use God merely as a convenient explanation of things we don't understand. Electricity, for example, was around in the world long before people understood it (and some say that it is still not really understood) and was thought to be evidence for all sorts of things. Now we know it has a natural explanation. As scientists learn more about the nature of time, they may well find better explanations for some supposedly inspired prophecies.

However, more important for us is the *nature* of prophecy. Is prophecy simply a foretelling of the future? Is any clairvoyant entitled to be called a prophet? Of course, there was an element of foretelling in prophecy, but it was by no means the dominant or mystical element which it is often claimed to be.

> Not everyone who says something definite about the future is a prophet. Prophets are distinguished from mere soothsayers in that they base what is impending upon the present, drawing their conclusions from the moral behaviour of the people around them.[31]

Klaus Koch draws a very important distinction between 'mere soothsayers' and prophets. The Hebrew prophets passionately believed that ungodly living would bring harsh consequences. They would see these consequences as God's 'judgment', a concept beyond the scope of this chapter, but which we shall look at later. Now we know that internally corrupt societies are more vulnerable to misfortune, be it military attack, famine or epidemic, than just ones are – for all kinds of definable reasons. So it was natural that, when Amos saw the deplorable lack of justice in the country, he would expect trouble to come, and would not have to look far to see the signs of it. Many of the prophecies of this kind are simply a reading of the signs of the times, from a religious standpoint. There was always a rising empire somewhere within a spear's throw and it would not take a military genius to predict that a state weakened by injustice, with the dissent and low morale that creates, would be vulnerable to attack. So the prophecy would be made that, unless the internal situation were redressed something called the 'enemy from the North' (or wherever it happened to be) would be upon them. We might well regard these prophecies as inspired, and as 'the word of the Lord', but not in the simplistic literal sense which is often used.

Then of course, when the nation was conquered and enslaved there was another function for prophets. They had to keep hope alive. So this time they would be on the lookout for signs of hope – of redemption. In such a situation, Isaiah sees the pagan king Cyrus as an unwitting instrument of

[31] Klaus Koch: The Prophets Vol. 1 (SCM 1982) p.2

God's purpose, and proclaims hope to the captive people on that basis. Situated in a crucial position on well-used trade routes, people with an interest in current affairs would be reasonably well informed and, of course, would see it all in the light of their understanding of God: a God of justice and mercy who punishes his people for being unjust and cruel to one another but always eventually restores them.

Of course, the prophets did much more than simply commentate upon the cycle of boom and slump in the nation's spiritual economy. They also had a vitally important role in offering alternatives. The prophet Isaiah, for instance, uses the figure of the 'suffering servant' in order to point to a better attitude to power. He calls the nation to commit itself to loving service, and be prepared to pay the price of real love. In this way they will become a light to the nations around them; a beacon of hope to which eventually all peoples will rally. And that brings us neatly to the next consideration.

If this view of the prophets is correct, how could they possibly have forecast with such uncanny accuracy the coming and the mission of Christ? Surely, they *must* have had direct revelation. Well, of course, what I said earlier still holds. Even if we accept these prophecies to be conscious statements about Jesus, we still have more than one way of explaining how the prophets came to have such visions. We need not use God to explain them. However, that is not enough on its own.

I have already referred to the Servant Songs in Isaiah. It is perfectly reasonable to believe that Isaiah was conscious only of the present situation. He offered a nation preoccupied with 'power' and 'success' a different image of those things. He pointed to the power of suffering love as a better way to relate, and he said that those who patiently endured, and did not (as Paul was later to say) return evil for evil, would eventually be vindicated. There are then at least two good reasons why this should appear as so accurate a foreshadowing of Jesus.

Firstly, if Isaiah was right, then it is surely only to be expected that that was the way Jesus would choose: the path of suffering love. It is inconceivable that the redeemer of creation should seek to identify with the world's images, rather than those which God endorses.

Secondly, of course, we must remember that Jesus was himself steeped in the biblical traditions of his day. He would know the prophets extremely well and, again, it is hardly surprising that he should see himself as the fulfilment of those prophecies and seek to live by the truths they reveal.

It is still of course absolutely right that we should regard those passages as 'inspired' and see in them revelations about the nature of Christ and of God. That does not need to mean that Isaiah had some knowledge of a man who was to live several centuries later, or of the manner of his death.

But this will not do, will it? The New Testament writers clearly saw Jesus as the literal fulfilment of the prophecies. And if I then say that they could be expected to do so, coming as they did from that kind of tradition, it will be pointed out that there are some very specific prophecies indeed which appear to have been fulfilled in Jesus. The evangelist Matthew is particularly well known for this. He cites prophecies of, among other things, the virginal conception of Christ, the flight into Egypt, the slaughter of the innocents and the eventual settling of the holy family in Nazareth. A brief look at those four examples is revealing.

> All this took place to fulfil what had been spoken by the Lord through the prophet: 'Look, the virgin shall conceive and bear a son, and they shall name him Emmanuel,' which means, 'God is with us.'[32]

This refers us back to Isaiah, and what do we find?

[32] Mat 1:22-23

> Therefore the Lord himself will give you a sign. Look, the young woman is with child and shall bear a son, and shall name him Immanuel. He shall eat curds and honey by the time he knows how to refuse the evil and choose the good. For before the child knows how to refuse the evil and choose the good, the land before whose two kings you are in dread will be deserted. The Lord will bring on you and on your people and on your ancestral house such days as have not come since the day that Ephraim departed from Judah – the king of Assyria.[33]

Isaiah has been sent to the terrified King Ahaz, and proceeds to give him a lesson in politics. 'Here,' he says, 'is a *young woman* who is pregnant. In the short time there is before her child is born and begins to grow up, the threats will have vanished. So stop running around like a headless chicken and get on with living as God wants you to, because it's *God* whom you need to be thinking about.'

According to which translation he was using, Matthew could easily find the words 'young woman' rendered 'virgin', and so far so good. What he could not do, however, was apply the text to Jesus *in context.* The last part of the quotation is nonsensical in those terms. It only makes sense in its own time and place. It may be possible to think in terms of the Holy Spirit revealing new layers of truth, but it certainly cannot be said that this text was specifically written to apply to Jesus.

Next comes the reference to the flight into Egypt.

> This was to fulfil what had been spoken by the Lord through the prophet, 'Out of Egypt I have called my son.'[34]

[33] Isa 7:14-17
[34] Mat 2:15

The 'prophecy' is of course from Hosea. In trying to call the people of Israel to repentance, the prophet portrays God as a wronged husband and, in this passage, parent. The people are reminded of God's amazing goodness to them *in liberating them from the Egyptians.* Hosea is speaking of something which happened centuries *before* him, and certainly has no idea of pointing forward to what is to come.

This brings us to the slaughter of the innocents, which is another classic piece of hindsight.

> Then was fulfilled what had been spoken through the prophet Jeremiah: 'A voice was heard in Ramah, wailing and loud lamentation, Rachel weeping for her children; she refused to be consoled, because they are no more.[35]

The quotation is accurate enough, but again it is out of context and the unfortunate fact is that Jeremiah, like Hosea, was referring to a past event. He was making no attempt to prophesy the future, but was speaking of what had already happened. Now again, in both these instances, as with the suffering servant, it may be possible and legitimate to say that these events had in some way foreshadowed the flight into Egypt and the slaughter of the innocents. It is also not only possible but vitally important to say that in their new context they contain new and valuable insights, and God may speak afresh through them. But the prophets' words cannot be held as prophecies, in simple terms, which say anything about either the nature of Christ or the status of scripture.

Finally, Matthew tells us that the move to Nazareth was also a fulfilment of prophecy:

> There he made his home in a town called Nazareth, so that what had been spoken through the prophets might be fulfilled, 'He will be called a Nazarene.'[36]

[35] Mat 2:17-18

[36] Mat 2:23

This is obscure. Unfortunately the text simply does not exist in the scriptures we now have. It could have been lost, but that seems strange if the scriptures were really infallible. More likely, as with the 'virgin' text from Isaiah 7, there is a dubious translation here which suits Matthew's purpose. There are texts which with a slip of a copyist's pen could easily have appeared this way, and opinions differ about which might have been used and what exactly it means, but scholars are fairly unanimous in saying that it does not refer to Nazareth.

This may seem all very threatening, but I would reiterate my basic position. I am writing from a position of belief in God and faith in Christ. The Bible is unique; I believe we can say it is inspired, but not that it was dictated. And serious though that may seem at first encounter, it does not in any way subvert the basis of faith. Nonetheless, this approach to scripture will be soundly denounced as 'lack of faith' or worse by those who are desperately trying to cling onto the shrub referred to in the previous chapter. They will go through agonies of torture in order to keep hold of what for them is essential to their existence. The answer of course is to let go. That means trusting God. It means letting God be God. It is not an easy thing to do, and the sense of insecurity when one does it is painfully real. In short, it takes more faith to let go than to hang on. Those of us who have done so, however, will testify that we did not find ourselves smashed to bits on the rocks. Rather, having let go of the idol of scriptural infallibility, we have found ourselves free to relate to God in new and exciting ways.

Letting Go

Let us at least contemplate letting go: ask ourselves what it would mean if we were to accept that the Bible, while inspired, is not infallible; that it contains the writings of innumerable human authors whose fallibility is sometimes all too evident. The result, I am convinced, would be that we should then be free to admit that in those stories about David, to which I referred earlier, the writers were interpreting the events according to their own agendas. They were attributing to God their own values and instincts, and perhaps sanctifying their own blood lust and xenophobia at the same time. The question then arises as to how God should respond to that. Should he allow 'his' book to be tarnished in this way, or should he do something about it? What does it say about God, if he does not?

The *God in control*, the God who holds the string, would either prevent this error or delete it from the manuscript before it got to publication. However, I have already said that I do not believe in that God. What I am now required to do is to ask how the relational God, to whose mast I have nailed my colours, would respond. If God is God, then there is no situation – and no error – which he cannot turn to creative purpose. The kind of passages I have cited still contain important truths about how people think, work and relate. The way the biblical writers sometimes use characters such as king David to sanctify their bloodlust tells me nothing about God, but a great deal about myself and my fellow human beings. It reminds me how easy it is to convince myself that whatever I want is actually God's will.

The point is that we might well be able to say that God speaks through scripture without having to say that he wrote it in the first place, but there is an objection of course. If what I have said about writers imposing their own agendas on their writing is accepted, then we are saying that the accounts are true but have been misinterpreted, which still leaves a bigger and thornier problem. What about the increasing number of writings which are regarded by scholars as simply having no basis in fact whatsoever? Many respectable scholars will openly say that favourite characters such as Noah, Jonah, Job, not to mention Adam and Eve, never actually existed. This is not simply a matter of how a story is interpreted; it is apparently being said that some stories simply are not factual. Surely we cannot say that God has allowed blatant untruths to be perpetuated in his name? Of course, if God has chosen to limit himself to working through relationships, then we could say that that is part of the price. He is bound to be misunderstood and misrepresented. However, that is not the whole answer by any means.

Truth and Fact

The nub of the problem is the confusion of truth and fact. Contrary to popular belief they are not precisely the same thing. It is a fact that I brushed my teeth this morning. No one is likely to want to debate the point, or to delve into the deeper meaning of the statement. It is simply a fact. On the other hand, there is truth in Aesop's fable of the hare and the tortoise. Few people would believe it as fact, but the truth is plain to see: that complacency is dangerous. So we may say that statements that are not factual can be full of truth, i.e. truth-full.

The stories of Job, Jonah and the rest are full of profound truth; so much so that centuries of careful study by countless people have not exhausted them. One might well say that it matters not a bit whether the characters themselves ever existed. What better way to proclaim the universality of God's love, to a nation only too familiar with exclusivism and xenophobia, than to tell the story of Jonah? Everyone loves a story, and not very many at all love a sermon. The storyteller will hold his listeners' attention and engage their imaginations infinitely better than the most skilful preacher. Surely it is to be expected that a wise, all-knowing God would have inspired people to tell stories rather than preach sermons? And if he did so, should he be particularly concerned to tell us which is which? Let us take for example the parables of Jesus. Was there ever a Prodigal Son? Was the story about the Samaritan on the Jericho Road (Jesus never called him 'good') factual? Which king was served by the unforgiving servant of Matthew 18:23-35? Jesus never actually said that any of these stories were parables, but we rightly accept them as such and do not trouble ourselves about how much connection they may have had with real events. We do not say that Jesus was lying, or that the stories are of less value because we think they are not 'true'. So cannot the God who is the same yesterday, today and forever choose to use similar techniques at other times and in other places? The reason Jesus never said whether these stories were parables, of course, was that it was supremely unimportant; it was the *meaning* which mattered. Similarly, with the creation stories, we have two different accounts, both of which are valuable images of the relationship between God, humanity and creation as a whole. These powerful stories have not one simple meaning, but many interweaving layers, and the presence of different accounts helps us to taste a little of the richness of this. It is meaning – not literalness – which matters. So why do we argue and tie ourselves in theological granny knots over the historicity of – for example – a man called Daniel, when what really matters is what we can learn from him?

Human insecurity

The desire for an infallible scripture springs from the same seed of insecurity which makes the *God in control* model so attractive. It offers us certainty in an unstable and unpredictable world. As long as we are convinced that God manipulated the biblical writers, and overrode their freedom, we can believe that he is in control. More fairly, we can be assured that something is certain. As we have already observed, the desire for certainty is a perfectly understandable thing. Unfortunately, however, if God will turn human beings into puppets in order to create an infallible book by which to manipulate future generations, then he is very likely to turn us into puppets as well whenever it suits his purpose. I believe that God worked with the biblical writers in the same way as he works with us: by relationship, relying on the persuasive influence of love rather than the power of coercion. I believe he loved them so passionately as to allow them their freedom, even at the cost of his being misrepresented and caused to suffer. More than that, so great was his love that he actually wanted their contribution to be taken seriously. Why else use human writers at all, since God would clearly be capable of carrying out that task himself perfectly well? The biblical literalist, I believe, must begin from a different concept of God: a God who is determined to be in control to the extent that he virtually turns people into robots. This is a God who uses people, manipulates them, ultimately regards them as tools in his hands. If we are to believe in a God who takes human freedom seriously, and wants a genuine, open relationship with us, then for that reason, even if there were no other, we cannot take a literalistic view of scripture.

I recognise that the argument of the 'slippery slope' is a very convincing one. If we once begin to accept that any part of scripture may not be literally factual, where will it end? Will we finish up with nothing but a set of rather wonderful allegories, parables and symbols? The only sure way to safeguard against this is to cling to the fundamental principle that scripture is infallible.

I fully understand this inclination, and would not want to be unnecessarily dismissive of it. Nonetheless, I have a problem. When I look at the emperor, I hear the crowd shouting about his wonderful clothes but my reason tells me he is naked. I am asked to violate my reason in order to feel secure. I am asked to hang onto the shrub by my fingertips, even though I can feel its roots giving way and I know that it cannot support me for much longer. It is time to take the decision of faith. It is time to let go.

CHAPTER FOUR

CREATION AND FALL

There is a story about a computer which was set the task of categorising and cataloguing the books in a library. To the dismay of the library authorities, it simply created a completely new category for each individual book on the grounds that no two were precisely the same and each had its own unique place in the scheme of things. The opposite tendency might perhaps be represented by my desk top on which there is usually a large pile of papers and books. My somewhat lame excuse for this is that I know where to find everything since there is only one pile in which to look . . .

In talking about God the creator, one really needs to think almost simultaneously about creation and fall. It is very easy to be tempted into either of the errors highlighted above, but the main tendency in traditional thinking has been toward the former. We look at the stories in the first chapters of Genesis, and we see an apparently clear pattern: the world was created in a state of perfection; temptation brought about the fall, and ever since then we have been struggling to climb a greasy pole back to God. Thus we keep the events of creation and fall tidily pigeonholed and analyse each as though it had little (other than cause and effect) to do with the other.

But the reality surely is that these are not neatly separable events but are two aspects of a continuing process, a developing relationship between God and the universe he has created. So rather than devote a separate chapter to each I have chosen to examine them together – in the context of the whole weave of which each is a strand, which is God's creative activity.

Before proceeding further, it would be good to summarise the discussions of earlier chapters, and identify the principles which have emerged, since they will be fundamental to the consideration of the doctrines and issues which follow.

- *God* is love. Because he loves us he wants us to be free and, most of all, to relate to him in freedom. Our response to God's love must be free or it would be meaningless. So he seeks to work by influence, by persuasion, rather than by coercion or manipulation.

- *Faith* in such a God is part of our free response. We are not to be bribed by simplistic rewards ('Have faith and everything will be well'); instead, we are called on a journey – called to commit ourselves to God without any absolute guarantees and to share in the risk of creative love. This is much more than simple belief or knowledge.

- *Scripture* is a collection of writings by people of faith. It is the product of their free relationships with God, and as such expresses their weaknesses and their misunderstandings as well as their great strengths and their piercing insights. We might describe it as inspired and certainly unique, but not infallible since God took the writers' relationship with him too seriously to override their fallibility. However, even when the human writers have got it wrong God is great enough to speak even – or especially – through their mistakes. The writers used the idioms and styles of their time and, in order to express what is beyond the reach of any literal language, they freely used imagery and metaphor. All this means that the important question as we read their texts is not, 'Is this literally true?' but 'What does this mean?'

In all this we have been seeking to 'let God be God' for us, and not to confine him within the idolatrous human concepts of power and divinity which might make us feel secure, but at the cost of stunting our growth.

So in considering creation, before we turn to the biblical material, it would be interesting to speculate a little on the question of what we might expect from a God such as this in the act of creation. It would seem likely that at least the following four points would emerge.

- God would want to have a relationship with creation, and not merely to make it and forget it.
- God would want that relationship to be the result of creation's *free* response to his love.
- God would seek at the earliest opportunity to enable creation itself to participate in the creative process, as part of the relationship.
- All this would involve some degree of self-limitation by God, in order to avoid imposing himself upon creation thereby invalidating the partnership.

So now we must ask what it means for God to be creator. The creation accounts in Genesis 1 and 2, along with that of the Fall in Genesis 3, have come to be represented as articles of faith in some quarters. One's whole theological position is thought to be summed up by whether or not one 'believes in creation'. Of course everybody believes in creation – it is difficult for most of us not to believe in something of which we are so obviously a part, and in which our whole existence is bound up. The question is really what one believes *about* creation.

Two conversations illustrate the polarisation which is always a danger in these discussions. In a programme about the role of church schools in education, a radio reporter was interviewing a teacher from a fundamentalist Christian school. Asked about the teaching of science in the school, the teacher replied, 'Of course we teach about evolution. But we teach evolution as a theory and creation as a fact.' The other conversation was one I had with an avowed atheist who distinguished between the 'fact' of evolution and the 'myth' of creation. So there we have it. One must believe absolutely in one or other but the two are irreconcilable. It is that idea, propounded by fundamentalists of opposing beliefs (for rigid atheism is as much a fundamentalism as any other), which is more mistaken than either of the supposed polarities which it offers. In reality, neither position can be described as 'fact'. The best that can be said for the theory of evolution is that it is the most convincing theory about the development of life, in terms of the data currently available to us. It cannot be described as a 'fact' in its own right. Creationism is yet another matter; it is neither 'fact' nor is it really a scientifically plausible 'theory'. Rather, it is a credal position, a tenet of faith, adopted by people of particular religious persuasions. The only 'facts' we have about creation are the natural phenomena which we can observe: plants, animals, minerals, fossils etc., and even they are open to a variety of interpretations.

The reality is, then, that neither account of creation can be described as fact, and they are not mutually exclusive except if we wish to make them so. Let us look at the biblical stories and see what can be made of them.

'Where did I come from?'

That is the question which parents have traditionally dreaded, and some have answered better than others. It is the question which, in one form or another, all children seem to ask. Some do not seem particularly interested, for example, in how birds fly; others really are quite unconcerned about how cars work; but curiosity about our own origins seems to be in some way part of our humanity. This suggestion is reinforced by the deep need which many adopted children have to know about their 'natural' parents. Even when they have been brought up in loving homes and formed strong emotional bonds with their adoptive families, and even at the cost of finding out unpalatable things about rejection, neglect or even abuse in the past – even then, many people have a deep-seated need to know 'where they came from'. For some people, this fascination extends to the very origins of the universe or even of time itself. In one way or another, and to one extent or another, all of us seem to be concerned with the question, 'Where did I (or we) come from?'

So it is not hard to imagine that, long before ways were found of writing down the answers, people were wrestling with questions about the origin of the universe. There were many supplementary questions: What great power lay behind the formation of the earth, seas and skies? Was this power benevolent? Was it still in control? If so, why did bad things happen? Why was life so hard? Why was childbearing so painful? Why did people become ill? – but perhaps greater than all these questions, the one which still occupies philosophers today: Is there any *purpose*, any *meaning* to it all?

The natural response to such deep questions was, as we know, to tell stories. Maybe people could not find straight textbook solutions for these problems, but they could tell stories which might point towards ideas not easily expressed in other ways. We now know that such stories were developing in primitive cultures all over the world, and that they contained some features in common and others which were vastly different. It is not surprising that, in the course of a nomadic lifestyle and after being conquered and/or carried off into slavery by great empires of the period, the Israelite people should accumulate a good stock of myths from which to develop their own understanding of God's purposes.

So we see, for example, the influences of the Babylonian myths in the Old Testament writings:

> You divided the sea by your might; you broke the heads of the dragons in the waters. You crushed the heads of Leviathan; you gave him as food for the creatures of the wilderness. You cut openings for springs and torrents; you dried up everflowing streams.[37]

Here we see also the idea of the subduing of chaos, which is such a vital feature of the Genesis 1 story.

If the ideas proposed earlier about God and scripture are acceptable, then this is clearly a reasonable understanding of how primitive women and men wrestled with the questions of their origins. When they came to write these stories down, however, they wanted to do more than merely give an historical account of creation, and this is where we must distinguish very clearly between the myths of Babylonian folklore, which really amount to fantasy, or perhaps even fairy tale, and the more developed stories in Genesis which really fall better into the category of theological reflection. The writers of the latter wanted to express the conviction that the reasons why the world worked as it did were bound up in the hopes and dreams of its creator. Most of all, they wanted to show what their own place was in the scheme of things – how they *related* to God and to creation.

In view of what has been said about the relational understanding of God, it is right for us to believe that God was involved in this process, but we must think of him as working within the dialogue, rather than suppressing it; as guiding, helping, influencing but not imposing.

The mystery of creation

As soon as we begin to think about creation we, like those early thinkers, find ourselves facing a mystery. Jurgen Moltmann[38] uses the distinction between 'creation' *(bara)*,

[37] Psalm 74:13-15

[38] Jurgen Moltmann: God in Creation (SCM 1985) p.73ff

used in Genesis 1:1 and 'making' *(asah)*, used in the subsequent verses, to remind us that the act of creation is without parallel and can therefore be compared with nothing else. This immediately deprives us of categories for discussing it. There can be no analogies. Nothing comes from nothing. We are therefore – or so it appears – unable to begin thinking about creation. But this is not as futile a position as it may appear. It simply reminds us, very healthily, that we are dealing with ultimate mystery and, while there are indeed many things we can learn and say, we can never learn or say everything. Here we are on common ground with science. As several eminent scientists of such note as Sir Bernard Lovell, for example, have observed, they too have only been able to describe the *development* of the universe; the initial act of *creation (bara)* is shrouded in mystery and may always be so.

Having been reminded of that, it will not be inappropriate in the context of this book, to continue to use the verb 'create' in the sense in which we generally accept it, as we examine the scriptural accounts of the *making* of the world.

The incompleteness of creation

For a long time the first few chapters of Genesis were viewed as a clearly written account of a perfect world which went wrong and then had to be redeemed. That view is now much less generally held, but held it is in some theological quarters and must therefore be considered here. For now, I shall leave discussion of the fall to one side although, as I indicated earlier, we cannot separate it from creation quite so neatly as has been attempted. Let us look, though, at the story in Genesis 1 and see if we really do have so clear-cut a picture as is sometimes still suggested. An important image is offered in 1:2-4.

> . . . the earth was a formless void and darkness
> covered the face of the deep, while a wind
> from God swept over the face of the waters.
> Then God said, 'Let there be light'; and there

> was light. And God saw that the light was good; and God separated the light from the darkness.

The picture is of God bringing order out of chaos. Here is chaotic material (whose original origins are shrouded in mystery) which needs to be given order. So the first thing to happen is the introduction of light, and its separation from darkness. The process of separation (a process anyone who has ever tidied a study desk will know well!) goes on until verse ten. Now the basic requirements are in place (although order is not finally secure as we shall see) and God can begin to do the real work of bringing life into existence. So, what does God do? We might be excused for expecting a clinically precise approach; the carefully developed order must not at this point be disturbed. That is how *we* would work, which is only one small reason why it is a good thing we are not God – for we get something gloriously unexpected.

> Then God said, '*Let the earth put forth* vegetation: plants yielding seed, and fruit trees of every kind on earth that bear fruit with the seed in it.' And it was so.[39]

What an amazingly reckless invitation! Here, surely, is a truly relational God at work. He throws caution to the winds and joyfully invites creation to become part of the process! Anyone with even as little gardening experience as I have will readily acknowledge the risk of an invitation like this. The carefully introduced order is threatened from this moment. It does not need a snake, or a fruit or any other device. How is God now going to prevent chaos from returning? At what point will he reassert his authority, re-impose his will on creation?

In verse 20, God appears to be compounding the folly of verse 11:

[39] Genesis 1:11 (my italics)

> And God said, 'Let the waters bring forth swarms of living creatures, and let birds fly above the earth across the dome of the sky.'

So now we have the first blossoming of animal life. If the creation story continues as it has so far, then further chaos is only a divine invitation away.

> God blessed them, saying, 'Be fruitful and multiply and fill the waters in the seas, and let birds multiply on the earth.'[40]

The story continues, with God repeatedly calling life into being and inviting it to multiply. Anyone who has watched germs breed under a microscope will recognise that there is now imminent danger of chaos breaking free. This image would be familiar to the Hebrew storytellers who knew the Babylonian myth of the great sea monster chained to the sea bed, the lashing of whose tail caused fearful storms at sea as the waters of chaos raged and threatened to engulf the world again. Primitive humanity was only too well aware of the imminent danger of the return of chaos. Is it too much to think that such thoughts as I have expressed were in their minds as these stories developed? Of course the writer says, 'God saw that it was good', but that does not mean that it was tame!

Finally in the creation process comes humankind created – uniquely – *in God's image*. Jurgen Moltmann says of that idea:

> What it means for God is that in creation he does not merely want to recognise his work; he also wants in his work to recognise himself. The creation of God's image on earth means that in his work God finds, as it were, the mirror in which he recognises his own

[40] Genesis 1:22

> countenance – a correspondence which resembles him. As God's *work,* creation is not essentially similar to the creator; it is the expression of his will. But as *image,* men and women correspond to the creator in their very essence.[41]

Now we find God giving a new commandment which has not been included in the invitation to the rest of creation to reproduce.

> God blessed them, and God said to them, 'Be fruitful and multiply, *and fill the earth and subdue it;* and have dominion over the fish of the sea and over the birds of the air and over every living thing that moves upon the earth.'[42]

So the frail safeguard against the potential return of chaos to creation is the relationship between God and his human co-creators. The nature of the command suggests that creation is as yet far from complete. It may be perceived by the writer as good, but it is not complete and it is far from incorruptible. The abundance of competing animal and plant life, unchecked by any divine restraint, can only be 'subdued' by the responsible stewardship of humanity. This, I would submit, is what the story in Genesis 1 presents to us. It is a long way from the idea of a perfect, compliant and well ordered creation which for some inexplicable reason went wrong. Furthermore, it is easy to see that this is a description not merely of a once-for-all event, but of a continuing process. It is not to be taken literally; the story is not *fact*, but is full of profound *truth* about the creative relationship between God and creation which is still in the process of being formed. It will be observed that there is plenty of scope here for a

[41] Jurgen Moltmann: God in Creation (SCM 1985) p.77
[42] Genesis 1:28 (my italics)

theory of evolution to coexist with religious belief without too much conflict. Except, that is, in one specific area.

The problem with evolution

Where this interpretation of Genesis 1 appears to come most seriously adrift from the theory of evolution is with regard to the special status of humanity. We cannot, it is argued, have it both ways: either humanity is a kind of grown-up ape, who just happened to evolve as one of an infinite number of possibilities, or we were specifically and uniquely created for relationship with God. This is a powerfully persuasive objection, but it is by no means the last word on the subject.

In Genesis 1, as we have observed, the specific verb translated 'create' is used almost uniquely for the initial act of creation; that great mysterious work of God which neither theologians nor scientists have been able to penetrate. *It is, however, used again, to describe the creation of humanity.* The writer wants to say that there is something ultimately mysterious about humanity which distinguishes us from the animal kingdom. This is grounded in the mysterious verb *bara* and expressed in terms of the image of God. Neither of those things have been said of any of the animals. So far, the creationists would appear to have all the points on their side of the debate. The uniqueness of humanity goes right back into the undisclosed creative purpose of God, and is not inherited from anything else. Of course, we should expect, with the general approach this book takes, that the limitations of the contemporary culture – in which theories of evolution had no place – would show in the writing of the story. But that is not the only thing to be said.

In the Genesis 2 creation story, the writer is clearly aware of something mysteriously unique in humanity, especially in our relationship with God, but also wants to make the point about our continuity with creation. So the two ideas are held together in verse seven:

> . . . then the Lord God formed man from the dust of the ground, and breathed into his nostrils the breath of life; and the man became a living being.[43]

The writer has God do two quite unique things. First of all, God actually dirties his hands. He 'formed man from the dust of the ground'. This intimate involvement is not described in terms of any other aspect of creation, and it can be understood in terms of God's using *the whole of creation* in the formation of humankind. Secondly, God breathes the spirit of life into humankind. So humanity is clearly marked as being distinctive, yet our continuity with (and dependence upon) the created order is also emphasised.

Both these points are brought out by John Weaver. Citing the Christian biologist R. J. (Sam) Berry's book, *Adam and the Ape,* Weaver argues that there is no biblical basis on which to oppose evolution.

> The fundamentalist Christian reaction against evolution does not have a scriptural warrant, and behind the view of a separate creation of humanity there are two fallacies in particular, as Berry rightly identifies. Firstly, it implies that God does not use the whole of his creation for his purpose. Secondly, it requires our relationship with God to be controlled genetically, as genes must be created to enable response to God; but the Bible excludes such a possibility, affirming the freedom of human response and the gift of Sonship that follows response.[44]

This second point is an important one. If God created instantaneously a new set of genes designed to be responsive

[43] Genesis 2:7
[44] John D. Weaver: *In the Beginning God* (Regent's Study Guides, 1994) p.98

to him, then that not only cuts us off from the rest of creation but also predetermines our response and denies us our freedom. What, though, of the qualities which specifically mark us out as human?

> The Genesis story bears witness to the emergence of a moral consciousness together with a sense of guilt about transgression; Adam fails to trust the purpose of God for human life and realises that he has failed (Genesis 3). Perhaps the 'critical point' of human development that anthropologists mark as the shift into settled existence coincides with the emergence for the first time of the sense of moral responsibility in relationships, which we discern as a mark of being truly persons; if so, we may see this development as being under the guidance of the Spirit of God who was deeply at work in the creative and evolutionary processes.[45]

This of course does not squash all argument, and that is right and proper. Theologians of most persuasions will say that there are flaws, from a theological point of view, in the theory of evolution. However, that is a long way from dismissing the whole theory and in my view not sufficient reason to resort to a literalistic interpretation of scripture which seems to me to create more problems than it solves.

THE PROBLEM OF EVIL

The problem with which any theology of creation must wrestle is that of the presence of evil in the world. As suggested earlier, the difficulty with the *God in control* model is that it ultimately makes God responsible for evil. That is

[45] John D. Weaver: *In the Beginning God* (Regent's Study Guides, 1994) p.95

just one of the reasons why I find that model of God unbelievable. At this point, I must recognise a very real danger. It is only too easy for someone who is not suffering in any very significant way to dismiss the evils of the world, which bring immense pain to countless people, with some clever theory. That is most certainly not what I intend to do. Neither am I attempting to provide a quick answer for use in pastoral crises. A necessary consequence of believing in a relational God is that there is no quick fix for anything. In relationships, sometimes the only answer to someone's pain is to share it, and to do so at immense personal cost; we shall be thinking about that later. However, we do need to consider, as dispassionately as we are able, whether there are any pointers towards better ways of understanding the evil in the world. And those of us who are not weighed down by it in the way some others are have perhaps the opportunity – and therefore the responsibility – to do that.

One way of understanding evil has been to personify it. Evil is presented as something tangible, even 'personal', a positive force imposing itself upon the world. There is value in this idea, for it tells us that the whole is greater than the sum of the parts. The classic Christian example of this is the crucifixion where the sum of a few very ordinary sins was the horrendous evil of Calvary. I shall return to this in discussing the atonement. The idea that evil is a positive force which can and does develop a momentum of its own is one we should not dismiss but keep in the forefront of our minds. However, this does not mean that we have to go to the extent of actually believing in some kind of evil counterpart to God. I said earlier that the idea of an eternal force of evil is out of line with Christian thinking which recognises only one eternal power in the universe. This being so, then we have to find ways of explaining the presence of evil in a world created by an entirely good God. I tried to show in chapter one[46] that there are fatal flaws in the traditional idea of a supernatural

[46] See p.23f

being, call it Satan, the devil or what you will. How such a person came to fall from grace – or to exist at all in a graceless state – is hard to explain without doing violence to the nature of God. We need to seek other explanations, and there are a number of ways we may begin to do this.

Light and darkness

When I was a child, I used to think that there was some substance called darkness. I had a mental image of some sort of celestial figure who came into the world at a predetermined time each day and scattered it around. Of course, there would have to be someone else, or perhaps the same person, who came into the world next morning and either gathered it all up or scattered light to dispel it. I never got so far as working that idea through.

If it is said that that sounds ludicrous, then I do not feel in the slightest offended, because of course that is precisely what it is. It is generally known now why the sky darkens at night and brightens again in the day. There is no such 'thing' as darkness. The only objectively existing thing is light. The darkness descends because the earth *turns away* from the light.

Now that does not mean that the darkness is unreal. Neither does it mean that we should underestimate its perils. Unpleasant things, both planned and accidental, happen in the darkness, and there is no doubt that the darkness is 'real'. It just is not a 'thing' in its own right. Light exists. It can be analysed. Scientists can identify the separate colours which go to make up white light. It can be used as a source of energy and a means of communication: modern telephone lines carry thousands of messages along a single fibre optic, by using light rather than electricity. Light is objectively real. The darkness we know at night is the absence of it.

That, I would suggest is a perfectly coherent view of evil. It is real. It is destructive. But it has no objective existence of its own; it is the absence of good. I must repeat that this should not result in our failing to take it seriously. Sin is a reality in the world, and I do not belittle it. Evil deeds, feelings and impulses are real and they cause untold misery. But they are the result of a turning away from the good, rather than an actual force of evil. There is only one objectively existing force in the universe, and it is supreme. It competes with no other. Its name is God.

The problem is that, precisely because God desires free relationship, the world has always been free to 'turn away'. Let us look at the Bible's classical account of how that happened.

The fall of humanity

The writer of Genesis 2 has a problem; more of a problem than the writer of chapter one. In that chapter, the possibility of a return of chaos was always there, but in chapter two God is much more in control. Creation itself is not as free; only humanity is free. So how did they come to fall? However, if we look carefully we find that the possibility is again built into this creation myth.

Why did God plant the tree of the knowledge of good and evil? Would you have done so, if you had been God? I don't think I should have done so; I like my own way too much. I think I should have left it out. Then what would the outcome have been? Creation would have been 'perfect' in my estimation. Adam and Eve would have loved me (because they could not do otherwise); they would have looked after the garden well (because they could not do otherwise); and they would always have known their place in the world (because they could not do otherwise). They would have loved each other (because they could not do otherwise), and . . . but this is becoming tedious.

And tedious is precisely what it would have been. The trouble is that Adam and Eve are birds in a gilded cage. As long as they do not know any differently, as long as they do not know good from evil, as long as they do not know how to rebel, how to say 'No' to God, there will be constant 'peace' and creation will be undisturbed. That is the kind of universe which you or I might well have created. What a good thing we never had the opportunity.

The writer of Genesis 2 knows that the 'birds' must be free. So there in the garden are two things, *both of which are part of creation*. There is the tree, from which they are told not to eat (and any psychologist could have told God what the result of that would be . . .) and there is the snake. Now the snake is often said to be the devil, but let us think about it a little more. We find it in the perfect garden, *before* the fall, identified as one of the creatures God had made. There is no suggestion that it is a malevolent influence from outside; quite the contrary. So the writer – like the writer of the first account – is saying that the seeds of the fall were present within creation itself; that God had designed creation for freedom.

There then follows a story which would be wonderful if we read it as it is, and not through the tinted spectacles of our own prejudices. A lot of people fear snakes, regarding them as sinister, and 'everyone knows' that women are a bad influence on men, and so the story is misused. But if we look with fresh eyes we see a much truer picture of the human condition. Suddenly we find free human beings refusing to take responsibility for their actions. 'Not my fault,' says Adam, 'the woman tempted me.' And we can surely hear the justified protest of women to the effect that men have almost always tried to blame them for virtually everything. Eve's response is no better than Adam's. She blames an animal, a form of life to which she is supposed to be superior. The poor snake, of course, has nowhere to turn. The buck stops right there. It is not the eating of the fruit which has caused disharmony in creation, but rather the failure of humanity to take responsibility for its own actions. As long as that is the case – as long as people refuse to accept their God-given responsibility for themselves, each other and the created order – there will be disharmony in creation. Treating the story as literal for a moment, for the sake of speculation, we may ask what might have happened had Adam and Eve each readily admitted their responsibility. Might not the whole relationship between humanity and other life have been utterly different?

So the fall of humanity – the turning away from the light – had disastrous consequences for creation as a whole. We only now have to look around us to see this as a present reality. As more and more of the planet is covered with concrete so that we can worship our cars; as species of animals are hunted to extinction or exploited by the food industry; as valuable resources are wasted to keep the rich rich and the poor poor; as whole countries are laid waste in the search for yet more resources, we certainly do not need to look very hard to find the consequences of this broken relationship.

We may, then, say of the fall what has already been said of creation (indeed we can hardly say it of one *without* saying it of the other): that it is not a single, unique event in history but an everyday occurrence. Once again, the biblical writer has given us a kind of parable about ourselves and our relationship not only with God but with the rest of creation.

But this alone is not an adequate response to the problem of evil, is it? We are also aware of the suffering caused by what are termed 'natural' disasters: by volcanic eruptions, floods and mud slides, by hurricanes and earthquakes, famine and drought. Is it really enough to lay all this at the door of humanity? Or is there something else about creation which we have not mentioned?

First of all, I would agree that the fall of *humanity* is not enough to account for natural disasters of that kind; it is arrogant to say that it is. However, before leaving this particular point there is one more thing to be said.

When an earthquake happened in Los Angeles, a few people died; when a very similar event occurred in Iran, thousands upon thousands died. Why? When there is a massive crop failure in the United States we do not get the same pictures on our screens as when it happens in the horn of Africa. Why? When large areas of Britain, America or Europe are flooded, generally we survive. When the floods hit the plains of Bangladesh, thousands perish. Why? The answer is that, much as we might like to put all the blame on God, it is not natural disasters in themselves which kill, but poverty. In those areas where most wealth is concentrated, there are the resources to deal with emergencies. There are reserves of food, buildings are designed to withstand shocks better, and so on. Most of the 'natural disasters' are probably not caused by human sin. I say 'probably' for we have for too long been pushing our technology beyond our capacity to control the consequences, and who knows what bitter lessons we may learn in the future? But if we accept that the earthquakes, floods or whatever are not in themselves the fault of humanity, we must nonetheless take responsibility for the severity of the *consequences*. Especially so in this age when most natural disasters are predictable.

Having said that, I recognise that it does not adequately address the question about the existence of evil. So we need to look elsewhere for some further possibilities.

The living world

I remember watching a television programme with the above title. It was part of a series which I was not usually able to watch, but the episode I did see gave me food for thought, including as it did dramatic pictures of volcanic activity. It was splendid stuff, but one could not help wondering how it would be to be trapped in the middle of all that, as people and animals all too often have been. In ways I cannot adequately put into words, I was brought face to face with the mixture of splendour and pain which is the ongoing creative process. I have already stated at some length that I believe creation is still incomplete. The Genesis 1 story introduces human life to creation before it is complete and portrays a world which is good, but which is certainly not finished. So as I watched the programme, in full colour, I felt I was receiving a glimpse of what an awesome idea that was. There was the continuing process of creation unfolding before my eyes, and I was not sorry to be safely in my armchair. This leads us on to consider an idea which may at first seem a little strange.

It has been suggested that not only is humanity free, but in some mysterious way every element in creation shares a degree of freedom. Every atom, we might now say, has some degree (however tiny) of ability to respond to God for better or for worse. I remember a fellow student referring to this theory in a seminar and receiving the scornful response, 'Come on, now – do you think you could preach to a rock?' The student's response was in two parts. Firstly, no one is saying that *we* can get a response from a rock, only recognising the possibility – however remote – that God can. The mere fact that we are unable to get any response from apparently inanimate objects does not in itself preclude God from doing so. Neither does one need to be so simplistic as to think in terms of nervous systems and means of communication such as exist in animal life. The fact that communication *as we understand it* is impossible is not the conclusive point. Secondly, who said we were going to preach to it? It is unfortunate that in some church traditions the sermon has become not only the main (which would be bad enough) but even the only means of communication and so when we speak in terms of response to God someone inevitably thinks we have to preach! And then we wonder why the churches are emptying!

It would not be appropriate here to embark on a thorough exposition of process theology (which is what the ideas outlined above are called) – even if I were competent to do so, which I am not – but it is useful simply to touch on the basic theory. According to this, creation consists at the subatomic level of what have been described as 'entities', each of which is able to attain a degree of 'satisfaction' by its response to God. Thus we can think of the whole of creation as being free and able – to a greater or lesser extent – to respond to God's love. This idea, in a very crude form, is certainly present in scripture where it is often said that all creation joins in praise to God; the mountains skip for joy and so on. And of course I have already focused upon the images in Genesis 1 where the whole of creation, before humanity is

– so to speak – a gleam in its Father's eye, is called to respond to God's invitation. So the process theologians' basic ideas can find plenty of support in traditional belief; and I am informed that quantum physics also gives possibility to those ideas. I hope however, that the reader will allow me to rely on the opinions of others more qualified in that last area since, had it depended upon my scientific grasp, we should still be awaiting the invention of the wheel . . .

If we were to investigate process theology in depth, there would certainly be aspects of it which would be more difficult to accept[47], but that is not the purpose of this book. Notwithstanding any difficulties in the developed theologies, the basic idea has much to commend it. Not only humanity but all creation, in ways well beyond our understanding, has the capacity (however limited) to gain satisfaction by response to God and therefore also has the freedom to find that satisfaction in other ways – to turn away from the light.

We might see this tension in terms of the very healthy instinct for survival which seems fundamental to nature. There is in the world a passion for life, for its own sake and not simply because it 'achieves' anything. It is easy to see how this fundamentally good trait which is, at heart, a participation in God's passion for life can be distorted. Once any entity turns away from the light, the healthy and necessary desire to survive becomes a very unhealthy desire to dominate. Anything which *apparently* threatens is kept at bay or subjugated or, if the means are available, eliminated. The instinct for life *as such* becomes an obsession with *my* life. The irony is that there are countless people who will testify to just how unsatisfying this is. The 'satisfaction' which is sought in this way is destroyed by the very process of seeking.

So the basic insights of process theologians, very superficially touched upon here, give us not an answer but perhaps a way in to the problem of pain in the 'natural' world. However, there is at least one more thing to be said on

[47] See for example *The Creative Suffering of God* by Paul Fiddes (OUP 1989)

this subject. The somewhat understandable assumption that anything which causes suffering must be evil cannot go unchallenged. Phenomena such as earthquakes, hurricanes and so on are certainly painful, but they may also be part of the evolutionary process by which, in a much longer view than we generally take of things, the requirements for life are provided. We shall be looking again at the question of whether pain can be thought of as positive in this way, later in this chapter.

The whole of creation, and not just humanity as we arrogantly assume, is being constantly called to respond to God, and each entity invited to live 'for creation' rather than 'for itself'. So what we are seeing is creation not *in being* but in the awesome process of *becoming* as God offers life, and the created order in its most basic elements responds by free acceptance or rejection of that call. We shall return to this later in the discussion of miracles.

Images of God the Creator

'Natural' theology

The warmth of the sun for pardon,
the kiss of the breeze for mirth;
you are nearer God's heart in a garden
than anywhere else on earth.

That little ditty expresses a way of looking at creation which I find offensive. Why? Because it is not true. It is certainly true that there are many examples of God's works in a garden, and I would be the last to deny that one can find communication with God easier in the tranquillity of a garden than in the bustle of a busy street or on a motorway. But the rhyme which I quote is saying something different: 'nearer . . . than *anywhere else on earth.*' The reason I find that offensive, primarily, is that it demeans humanity. There are many texts which could be quoted which clearly express the belief that God is most closely encountered in humanity – and especially, if Matthew 25:31-46 is to be believed, in *suffering* humanity. We shall certainly look at this claim more closely later on, but it is important, if we are to take seriously the idea of God as creator, that we do not sentimentalise creation. We must keep in mind that there is a distinct difference between creation as God's *work* and humanity as his *image* – a distinction of which Moltmann reminded us earlier.

The Christian claim is that God supremely revealed himself not in mountains, fields, oceans or animals but in a *person*. And it is through *personal* knowledge of God that salvation is possible. The natural order is not to be dismissed; it is undoubtedly the work of God. But it is not to be seen as the *image* of God. More importantly, it is not to be used as an idol to worship in place of its creator. If we want to see images of God the creator we must look to humanity. There we shall find many vivid images, of which I propose to consider just two that are particularly helpful in terms of our relational model: God as creative artist, and as Mother of creation.

The creative artist

When I was at school I was obliged, like all pupils, to study art. It was a great relief both to the teacher concerned and to myself when the time came for me to choose my options for 'O' Level G.C.E. and I was able to drop the subject! Still, excruciating though my efforts were for all who had to look at them, the lessons did serve to teach me something very important. That was because I was lucky in my teacher, who seemed to have a wonderful ability to bring some sort of order out of the worst imaginable chaos. She would look over my shoulder at the ghastly daub in front of me and, where a lesser person would have simply thrown it away and suggested I start again, she would respond quite differently. 'Let me see,' she might say, 'I think we can do something with that.' Then, before my incredulous eyes, a transformation would take place and my apparently worthless effort would acquire some degree of shape and meaning. What resulted would certainly never have been put on display, for this consummate artist was limited more than somewhat by her distinctly less creative partner; nonetheless, because of her ability to turn a sow's ear into a passable kind of purse (although definitely not a silk one!) something had resulted from all that effort – something which neither she nor I could have foreseen. Left to herself, she would have produced something infinitely better. Left to myself, I should have scrapped the whole thing in despair and never realised what possibility there was. I had the enormous pleasure of working with a truly creative artist. She, on the other hand, was severely hampered by the partnership, but made that necessary sacrifice because to a teacher of her professionalism *it was the partnership which mattered*. And she took the partnership, unequal though it was, with absolute seriousness. What resulted from our combined efforts had to include something of me, however inadequate that was and however much it distorted her contribution. That was the cost to her of being in partnership with her pupils.

I hope my drift is becoming clear. Left to himself, God would no doubt have produced a much more artistic creation than this one. On the other hand, had we been left entirely to ourselves we should probably have despaired completely well before now. If we accept the image of God as a creative artist, then we can see the world as being hopeful rather than hopeless. In such an unequal partnership it is hardly surprising that there is so much in creation which is not the best its creator could have produced if left alone to do so. But what does it mean for God to take this partnership with creation seriously? Once again, we come back to the issue of freedom. The contribution made by creation to its own becoming is only of real value if it is made freely. This means not only that creation is free not to respond at all to the invitation; it also means that creation is free to respond *ineptly*. It is easy to see examples of well-meaning ineptitude in creation. We know that in the human sphere the best of intentions can result in the worst of consequences. God's response in those circumstances is not to discard the result and start again, but to find ways of bringing something good out of the chaos.

Here we are in the fraught area of freedom and consequences. Freedom without consequences is illusory. It is patronising to say to somebody, 'Of course you are completely free, but I shall ensure that whatever you do has no consequences.' So it is in God's relationship with the world. If the contribution creation makes to this partnership is to be truly free, then both creation and creator must respect the consequences of that.

However, there is a thornier problem yet which this analogy raises. My art teacher was many things, but she was not omniscient. She had no way of knowing, until she looked over my shoulder, what my contribution to the artistic work of the class would be. One of the great joys of her creativity was precisely that something was happening which neither of us had anticipated. Here, it will readily be seen that there is a disjunction in our analogy with God as a creative artist. God, it will be objected, *is* omniscient. So how does any of this have any real value? Once again we are in danger of a patronising and dishonest relationship. God knows, we might say, exactly how things are going to turn out; whatever we do will make no ultimate difference, and so our life is really meaningless. We have raised this before, in chapter one, when thinking about the nature of God. Now we need to consider it a little more thoroughly. Is it at all meaningful to talk about God as having a *creative* relationship with creation if in fact we are simply working out a predetermined plan?

Looking back to when I was at theological college, I remember a sermon class where my preaching was to be assessed. The context of this was to be a family service where I had earlier begun to experiment with discussions rather than sermons. In the informal setting, they actually worked well and it seemed good to use this for my assessment. So the tutor duly arranged to be present to hear it. Of course, I was anxious that the resulting report should be a good one and the consequence was that I stifled the discussion. The report on the sermon class said that it was a good idea which hadn't worked because I had been too anxious to steer the discussion along predetermined lines, and so failed to allow the congregation fully to take part. I realised that, in my determination to impress the tutor, I had in fact patronised the congregation and stifled any creativity which there might have been in the process.

So is God taking creation's own contribution to the partnership seriously or not? This is an intimidating line of enquiry, for we seem to be in danger of saying that God is limited; that he does *not* know the final outcome of creation. And in saying that, we seem in grave danger of not letting God be God. But all is far from lost.

To begin with, there seems to be an idea that there is only one possible outcome which is acceptable to God. Creation must, in order to be perfect, eventually turn out in a particular way; anything else would be something less. But is it not strange that God should have so narrow a scope of possibility open? Is it not at least equally and probably more reasonable to suppose that an infinite God should enjoy infinite creative possibility? Since infinity is by definition unimaginable, however, let us merely say that there might be millions of possible forms which creation could take and still be perfect. Is it possible, then, that God knows what they are but chooses to leave open the question of which will finally materialise? Is it not even conceivable that he chooses not to know all the possibilities? The immediate response to this idea is that since God is omniscient it is impossible for him not to know, but it is a strange contradiction to defend the infinite power of God by saying that anything is impossible for him! Presumably, it is well within God's power to limit himself[48]; indeed, the whole argument of this book is based on a self-limiting God. If we can accept that God is free to limit himself, and that that is a sacrifice he chooses to make for the sake of creation's freedom and therefore for the sake of

[48] cf. Philipians 2:6

relationship, then the concept of God as a creative artist is an appealing one, and of course is completely congruent with the ideas proposed so far in this book, including the freedom of all creation. It does not satisfactorily answer the question of evil on its own; if it did there would not be a Christian religion for there would not be a cross. But it is part of the broader tapestry within which that event itself may begin to make sense.

Mother of creation

Here is another possible analogy, and one which is rightly gaining acceptance. It is at first a strange one to many of us, brought up as we have been on the masculine images of God. However, the Bible itself is not without feminine images. It is not surprising, given the way the Bible has developed, that masculine images are overwhelmingly more common, but that does not invalidate the feminine ones. On the contrary: given the overbearing weight of patriarchalism it is surprising that *any* feminine images have survived, and the fact that they have done so against such inestimable odds means that they have to be taken very seriously.

Before looking at some examples of this, we really should ask the question as to why there is such resistance to this idea. Those committed to a more literal approach to scripture will claim that Jesus called God 'Father' and he should have known, but it really is impossible to sustain that view with the general approach taken in this book. We have to look at the issue more carefully than that. Indeed, it is for those who oppose the idea to explain how God can be the source of all that is good (which presumably includes the feminine) if those attributes are not present within the Godhead. The traditional belief that in marriage two become *one flesh* must mean that masculinity and femininity are in some way complementary and both are part of the image of God in humanity. Let us look at some of the biblical images.

The prophet Hosea is well known for having portrayed God as a cheated husband. However, he also uses the image of an unappreciated and rejected parent:

> When Israel was a child, I loved him, and out of Egypt I called my son. The more I called them, the more they went from me; they kept sacrificing to the Baals, and offering incense to idols. Yet it was I who taught Ephraim to walk, I took them up in my arms; but they did not know that I healed them. I led them with cords of human kindness, with bands of love. I was to them like those who lift infants to their cheeks. I bent down to them and fed them.[49]

It is only because of the traditional images of God that we fail to see the maternal quality of this passage. God teaches her children to walk; she bends down to pick them up; she heals them; she leads them; but most of all, she *lifts them to her cheek*. Even in this century we ought to be able to see what a feminine picture this is. Happily there are more fathers who now relate in this kind of way to their children, but even in this comparatively liberated age (let alone in Hosea's time) we should probably have assumed the speaker was feminine, had we not known she was God!

I am aware that feminine pronouns tend to jar, but in the context of God as Mother, masculine ones seem quite inappropriate. Perhaps it would be worth taking a moment or two to consider why feminine pronouns should seem so strange, especially when the Wisdom of God in the Old Testament is frequently portrayed as feminine.

Another prophet, this time Isaiah, is much more specific in portraying God as feminine:

> For a long time I have held my peace, I have kept still and restrained myself; now I will cry out like a woman in labour, I will gasp and pant. I will lay waste mountains and hills, and dry up all their herbage; I will turn the rivers

[49] Hosea 11:1-4

> into islands, and dry up the pools. I will lead the blind by a road they do not know, by paths they have not known I will guide them. I will turn the darkness before them into light, the rough places into level ground. These are the things I will do, and I will not forsake them.[50]

This is a powerful passage indeed. The birthing imagery is explicit in the first verse, while subsequent verses go on to portray the agony of childbirth in terms which envelop creation. The laying waste of parts of creation is actually an expression of the pain of bringing it to birth. The joy of the actual birth itself comes subsequently: the blind will be led to the light, have their way lovingly cleared before them; they will never be forsaken. We may notice here some very clear similarities with the Hosea passage as the child is cared for and enabled to walk. God will never forsake the creation to which she has so painfully given birth.

The New Testament provides another insight, particularly appropriate after the crucifixion:

> We know that the whole creation has been groaning in labour pains until now; and not only the creation, but we ourselves, who have the first fruits of the Spirit, groan inwardly while we wait for adoption, the redemption of our bodies. For in hope we were saved. Now hope that is seen is not hope. For who hopes for what is seen? But if we hope for what we do not see, we wait for it with patience. Likewise the Spirit helps us in our weakness; for we do not know how to pray as we ought, but that very Spirit intercedes with sighs too deep for words.[51]

[50] Isa 42:14-16
[51] Rom 8:22-26

Here we see a particular value of the birthing image: the pain is shared by creator and creation. The act of giving birth is one which involves *shared* pain. The image, then, is not of God inflicting suffering on creation but of her actually participating in it. More than that, it is deliberately chosen as part of the process of bringing about life. This, it will be realised, is a much healthier view. It also exposes us to the idea of a creatively suffering God, and such an idea immediately rules out any suggestion that God actually inflicts the pain.

Our whole contemplation of the mystery of pain is affected by whether we think it is the pain of death or of birth. The former is a cause for despair; it is futile suffering with no end in sight except oblivion. The latter is real, and no doubt excruciating, and is undeniably dangerous; let no one – especially a male writer – romanticise the pain of childbirth. But I am assured that it is generally of a different order precisely because it is endured in hope.

Many parents will also see the connection with the whole business of building family relationships. In one sense the pain of actually bringing a child into the world foreshadows the pain to come in the future when the growing personality tests the parental love to the uttermost and the cost of keeping the hope of reconciliation alive is paid by the parent in patient, suffering love. This we shall shortly look at in greater depth under the heading of 'atonement'.

There is much more that can be said about this image of God as creator, and it would certainly repay further contemplation, but we have done enough for now.

It will be seen that both these images, that of the creative artist and that of the mother, are closely related. Both are useful in understanding something of what it means to believe in a relational God, rather than *God in control.*

From all that has been said, it may easily be seen that the doctrines of creation and fall are ways of speaking not of unique historical events but of a continuing historical reality: two strands which constantly interweave as God always and everywhere calls creation to a relationship of mutual self-giving love and the multitude of elements within creation, while often undoubtedly responding positively, also abuse their freedom to seek their own satisfaction at the expense of the wholeness of creation. The pain which results from this is shared by the creation itself and by its long-suffering, eternally loving mother.

That idea of mutuality should never lead us to think of ourselves as *equal* partners with God, of course; nonetheless, in order for us to be partners at all, God has chosen to limit the use of his power so that our response can be a free one. This freedom of response in which, to a greater or lesser extent, all creation shares, includes the possibility of *negative* response; only thus can it be true freedom. More than that, it means that the consequences of those negative responses must be allowed to follow since freedom without consequences is illusory. Further still, because we are created for relationship, the failure of one part of creation (or one person) may and does result in undeserved painful consequences for others. This enables us to see evil not as an objectively existing entity but as the absence of, or a turning away from, good – just as the descent of darkness each evening is the result of the world's turning away from the light. However even the results of that may be drawn into the process, redeemed by the power of suffering love, and incorporated into God's purpose. In this regard, two images of God are particularly helpful: as Creative Artist in partnership with his materials, and as Mother bringing creation to birth and fully participating in the shared pain of doing that.

The reader might have had an uneasy feeling throughout this chapter that what is being spoken of here as 'creation' is actually more like 'redemption'. The answer is, of course, that the distinction is necessarily blurred. In the biblical traditions, the creation of the world was seen in terms of its redemption from chaos. Primitive humanity, always fearful of falling into non-existence felt constant need of redemption from that state. Clearly, if creation and fall are continuing realities, then redemption must be that, also. Constantly falling away from God, we are always in need of redemption. And the very word 'redemption' of course suggests a cost, a 'buying back' of what is lost. We have seen that there is a monumental cost to God in holding open the relationship with creation. So it is easy to see how creation and redemption run together through the fabric of God's dealings with the world, in a way which makes them very hard to separate as tidily as we might like.

CHAPTER FIVE

THE CONTINUING RELATIONSHIP

In the last chapter, we considered the creative work of God, and saw it as a continuing relationship with creation. The question which must now be addressed is how this relationship is conducted and expressed on a day to day basis. After all, miracles seem to be examples of God's specific intervention in creation and prayer seems, quite literally, to ask for precisely that. So is there any room for such concepts if we are committed to belief in a God who works by relationship rather than by arbitrary intervention?

If we are, rightly, wary of the idea of an interventionist God, then the whole purpose of prayer is called into question. What are we hoping that the result of prayer will be? This of course applies in particular (although not exclusively) to intercessory prayer where there is an implied belief that God will act as a result of our prayers. If he will not, then what is the point of prayer? This relates closely to the subject of miracles which seem to make a case for intervention. Perhaps it is not possible to believe in miracles at all, without believing in a God who intervenes; and if we cannot believe in miracles then it would seem that prayer is pointless. Indeed, it would seem worse than pointless; after all, continually asking a friend or relative for something which he or she is obviously not going to give can only be damaging of the relationship we have with that person. So it seems appropriate to begin this chapter not with the subject of prayer but by examining the concept of miracle. Only after we have reached some workable understanding of that will it be fruitful to think about prayer. In other words, before we consider the means we ought to define the ends. Does God work miracles; and if not, what is the purpose of prayer?

It will be necessary to consider various common ways of understanding miracles, and see how consistent each might be with the concept of a relational God. Then, having arrived at a basic working definition, I propose to think about a number of different forms of prayer. It might help shed a little light on the subject if we begin by establishing the distinction between two rather important words.

Miracles: Intervention or Involvement?

I believe in miracles; I believe I have witnessed some. I say, 'I believe' since I am aware that others might not see those events in the same way as I do, of which more later.

In a church where I served, the idea was introduced of holding regular evenings to host a club for people with learning disabilities. The purpose of the 'Hand in Hand Club', which has existed for many years, is to encourage contact and better understanding between the general public and people with special needs. I arrived for the first of their visits to us to be greeted by a member of the church who candidly confessed to being there somewhat unwillingly. He had, he said, come simply out of a sense of duty, being unable to justify staying away, but he would be glad when the evening was over. I said that I appreciated not only his candour but his presence under those circumstances. Later in the evening, I saw him dancing with one of the mentally disabled club members, and displaying his enjoyment in a huge grin. As we cleared up after the evening, he commented that it was one of the best social events he could remember in the church. During a subsequent review of the venture, he told the church that his eyes had been opened, that he had received infinitely more than he had given, and the evening should be repeated. The club's visits to the church are now eagerly looked forward to by members of both organisations. Whether one regards that as a miracle depends, of course, upon one's point of view. One might regard it simply as the natural outworking of events, and interpret it purely in social and psychological ways, or it may be seen as what John Macquarrie calls 'the approach and self-disclosure of [God] to us.'[52] This ambiguity, as I shall argue shortly, is an essential feature of miracles. However, before pursuing that point further, let us turn to the fundamental problems with the whole idea.

A common – and perfectly reasonable – question on the lips of many contemporary people concerns a God who is believed to have endless power and is widely and often aggressively publicised as a miracle worker, but who yet signally fails to intervene in what seem to be the most deserving cases. If the stories we hear of miracles are true, then why does God not work a few more of them? According to a gospel story, Jesus was concerned about five thousand people who had missed a single meal, and yet global starvation now goes on unabated. Why does God not work a miracle or two there? Now, of course it is a bad argument simply to say that, because miracles appear not to happen whenever we expect, therefore they cannot happen at all. However, the kind of inconsistency to which I have referred must raise legitimate questions about the nature of God. As a colleague of mine put it, we have to conclude either that 'he would if he could, but he can't' or that 'he could if he would but he won't'. In other words, we either have an all powerful God who could change things and chooses not to because he doesn't care, or a compassionate God who longs to intervene and put things right but simply has not got the power to do so. Of course, we could leap to the apparently obvious conclusion and say that – since either of those alternatives cannot be God as generally understood – there cannot be a God at all and the whole structure of religious belief and commitment has been built upon a concept which humankind has created. As I have indicated a number of times, I do not believe that it is necessary to leap from the one caricature to the other.

[52] John Macquarrie: *Principles of Christian Theology* (SCM 1986) p.252

The question of whether we can believe in an intervening God is the main focus of this book, and I have tried to show that, in a crude sense, such a God is beyond belief. However, that is not to say that we cannot believe in a God who is *involved* and who makes a difference. Traditional Christianity specifically does make such a claim, and my main concern has been to show that we can believe in a God who is involved with creation and seeks to build relationships through which he may influence and change that creation without at the same time overriding its freedom. The consideration of God as Creator in the preceding chapter has made that very necessary distinction. Now we must ask whether there is room in that relationship for what we, following our forebears in the faith, have called miracles. And if there is not, then what do we make of the countless miracle stories in our tradition?

What is a miracle?

The normal usage of the word 'miracle' has to do with things which cause wonder, but in that case the view from Brecon Beacon or the scenery in South West Ireland could be termed miraculous, along with countless other examples around the world. However, no-one would seriously describe them as such, and so the definition of 'miracle' as something that causes wonder clearly will not do in the context in which we are considering it.

For similar reasons the use of the word to describe something which cannot be explained is also inadequate. There is no doubt that this is precisely how it was once used in religious circles, and often still is, but hindsight gives the lie to it since to Stone Age people the movement of the tides would presumably have been a miracle, along with many other natural events which we now understand. So today's miracle then becomes tomorrow's commonplace and we find this sort of miracle suffering the 'God of the gaps' effect as the scope for miracles decreases in proportion to our growing understanding. Miracles, along with the God who is credited with them, then get pushed into ever smaller and more remote gaps in our knowledge until we find it reasonable to suppose that there is no more room for either of them.

One of the very common ideas about miracles is as a reversal of natural law. However, there are at least two serious problems with this. Firstly, it relies very heavily, of course, on the *God in control* model and is therefore difficult to reconcile with the general thinking expressed in this book. Secondly, and perhaps more seriously, there is the not unrelated objection that it sets God against nature, rather than portraying him as working with it. So if we are committed to the basic understanding of God as relational it would be better to see whether there are better ways of speaking about miracles than this.

One way which has appealed to many people is the subjective one which says that they are actually ordinary events which are 'seen as' miracles by the eye of faith. This is a perfectly plausible idea, but the danger is of actually disqualifying the events from being called miracles. Virtually anything can be 'seen as' a miracle from *somebody's* faith position, so everything is a miracle to somebody. And if everything is a miracle, then nothing is a miracle. As W. S. Gilbert observed in his affectionate send-up of republicanism:

> When everyone is somebody,
> then no one's anybody! [53]

Nonetheless, this theory is not to be dismissed out of hand. For reasons already outlined in this book, matters of faith always have a degree of ambiguity about them. That is not simply because God respects our freedom and does not wish to compel belief, but also has to do with the very involvement of God in creation. The whole created order is 'in God', and every process within it is in some way (co-operatively or otherwise) intertwined with his purpose. It is not difficult to

[53] Gilbert and Sullivan: *The Gondoliers*

understand, therefore, that any event which manifests God's presence and activity will also be open to 'natural' explanation. So everything could be described as a miracle, and everything could be regarded as 'natural'.

The most usual definition of a miracle in religious circles, of course, is that it is an extraordinary event caused by a supernatural agency. If this is taken to mean a direct intervention of God in which the laws of nature are suspended or overridden, then there is obviously a problem and we are back to the *God in control* model again.

If we are committed to the concept of a relational God constantly at work in creation, calling creation into relationship but allowing it the freedom to refuse, then the popular idea of miracles is very difficult to hold onto. Furthermore, it is theologically offensive if it causes us constantly to be seeking after 'signs' and expecting God to bolster our deficient faith by jumping through hoops for us. However, we should be careful not to leap to the opposite conclusion and say that God cannot have any influence within creation; the whole of this book is devoted to arguing the opposite. Perhaps what we are seeking is some way in which the term miracle might refer to high points in God's ongoing relationship with creation, rather than arbitrary interventions. This idea is in no sense new, having been around for a very long time. It is suggested that miracles occur at moments when the activity of God breaks through the barriers which nature presents, and is revealed. This is nearer the mark but as it stands it invites a very powerful objection in that it sets God in opposition to nature. Surely, the counter-argument runs, if God is working within nature then it is when natural forces are strongest, not weakest, that events we call miracles are most likely to happen. However, that is to oversimplify the argument.

In the light of what has been said about creation it seems quite legitimate to believe that, as God constantly seeks to deepen his relationship with creation, there will be high points and low points in that relationship. Indeed, the very expression 'that relationship' is clearly inadequate referring as it does to an incredibly complex matrix of interweaving relationships involving and affecting every element in creation. As the relationships and interrelationships develop and change there will be moments when the degree of harmony between Creator and creation is such that extraordinary possibilities arise. At such moments, things may happen which – because of their unusual character – might be called miracles. Those events, however, far from being arbitrary interference by God against nature are in reality moments of unusual intimacy and oneness of God with nature. We all know that in any relationship there are high points and low points. The whole idea that God allows creation freedom must mean – as we have seen – the freedom to co-operate and the freedom to obstruct. Given the immense complexity of the created order, it is reasonable to suggest that at any given moment there will be elements in varying degrees of harmony with God's purpose and others more or less seriously at odds with it. At those moments of fullest harmony, events which may be described as miracles happen. John Macquarrie takes this sort of approach.

> God's presence and activity are everywhere and always; yet we experience these intensely in particular concrete happenings, in which, as it were, they have been focused.[54]

It seems reasonable, then, to regard miracles not as examples of God's arbitrary intervention in creation, but as moments of revelation of his continuous *involvement* within it. The more at one Creator and creation are, the more God's purpose will be accomplished. Those moments will obviously cause wonder and may be called miracles.

[54] John Macquarrie: *Principles of Christian Theology* (SCM 1986) P.252

The Miracles of Jesus

Macquarrie presents Jesus as the supreme miracle.

> From one point of view, Jesus represented simply another human life, the life of a turbulent innovator in the eyes of most who saw him. But to the disciples, this life was the focusing of the presence and action of God.[55]

Jesus himself was a classic example of what is good in the 'seeing as' argument, and the same must be said for the miracles he performed. For the people of the time, let alone for us, the evidence was not compelling, as the gospels themselves show in the repeated disputes which surrounded the miracles.[56] For us, two millennia later and after the Enlightenment, there are even more questions, some of which are outside the scope of this particular volume. However, there are some useful points to be made.

First of all, there was a common idea in Jesus' day that the ability to work miracles was evidence of special status or holiness; a common idea, but far from a universal one. In the present day, miracles are often used as supposed proof that God is at work; in the worst cases they are used to justify claims to Christian supremacy – religious one-upmanship. However, in these terms they 'prove' nothing, for in Jesus' own day there were many miracle workers who had no allegiance to him at all. Similarly, in the present day, 'faith' healing is a phenomenon much more widespread than any particular faith tradition. So if miracles prove anything about God at all, it must be that God is active much more widely and under a greater variety of names than most of us like to admit. It is always worth remembering that Jesus himself refused to reduce miracles to the level of circus tricks in order to 'prove' himself. The miracles were frequently referred to as

[55] John Macquarrie: *Principles of Christian Theology* (SCM 1986) p.253
[56] e.g. John 9:13-34

'signs' – especially by John – but this does not mean 'signs of who Jesus was'. They were signs of the kingdom of God: signs of what God is able to achieve in the transformation of people's lives, and of the society in which they live. An example of this is John's account of what he describes as Jesus' first 'sign' in Cana of Galilee.[57] The transformation of water into wine is a sign of the transformation of life from one based on adherence to the law to one lived by grace. The water jars were there so that the law could be observed, and clearly the observance of the law had been carefully provided for while the celebration of life and love had fallen a little short! By his 'sign', Jesus showed that God can transform legalistic religion into a celebration of life in all its fullness.

In the fourth gospel account especially, the word 'signs' is used in a special way. The miracles of Jesus pointed to a reality of which they were themselves part. Consider a signpost which points toward a particular town. That is all it does. In itself it has no connection with that town, which might be a huge distance away. On the other hand, the sound of an approaching carnival is a sign of a different type. The sign is part of the reality. So, when Jesus performed miracles they were not mere academic proofs of the existence of something beyond sight. The healing of the sick, the restoring of the outcast, the overcoming of greed and prejudice – all these things actually signified the presence of the new order to which they themselves belonged. Therefore, any kind of showmanship or coercive pressures upon people's minds would have been completely out of place.

This of course still leaves open the question of intervention. Whatever these miracles *meant,* the claim that they happened at all seems to mean intervention by God – the kind of contravention of nature which has already been rejected as unacceptable. So, how might these miracles now be understood?

[57] John 2:1-11

The first point is that the gospels were recorded in much the same sort of way the Old Testament came about; that is they were written down many years after the events themselves using a mixture of oral traditions and other writings. Furthermore, they are not intended to be simple factual narratives but are designed to convey *meaning*. To present them in a literalistic way as almost photographic evidence of specific events is to do them an injustice. All of this needs to be taken into account.

Secondly, we must see the miracles as issuing from Jesus' *relationship with God*, rather than from some kind of individual supernatural power. Indeed, we must go somewhat further. While we are very accustomed to recognising Jesus' special relationship with his Father, we are perhaps less used to thinking of his being also closely attuned to creation. Surely, though, the two must go together. To be close to the Creator, especially the kind of Creator we have considered in the last chapter, must by definition involve being close to the creation. In Jesus, therefore, we see someone almost uniquely at one with God and with creation. So is it too much to suppose that such a relationship as that would enable extraordinary things to happen? It may well be that in a few hundred years from now (or perhaps considerably sooner) science will have identified channels of energy and communication which are at present not even dreamt of but which can be used, albeit unconsciously, by unusually sensitive people. Many of us may know ordinary people who do not involve themselves in histrionics, but who seem to possess some sort of 'healing touch' which they cannot explain. Others may seem able to communicate telepathically with close relatives across distances, and yet others may find that their thoughts seem to be strangely effective in ways which baffle them. I do not refer here to bending spoons on television, or to people touching an orange dot in the hope of changing their lives or feeling better, but there certainly do seem to be channels of energy and communication which are mysteriously available to some people who cannot themselves account for the phenomena. I have every confidence that if the world lasts long enough these things will be explained in natural terms. To push God into those gaps, in a simplistic way, is to ask for trouble. However, if God is at work within creation then he is certainly involved in all of that.

Altogether, I firmly believe that Jesus was indeed remarkably in touch with God and with creation, sensitive not only to people but to his environment as a whole, to the extent that in his presence extraordinary things happened. That is quite consistent with the whole concept of God working by relationship, and with the possible understanding of miracles as high points in that relationship.

Miracles in the Church

We need to distinguish very carefully between unexplained and quite possibly miraculous events which happen in the context of caring communities (whether church or not) and the vulgar showmanship which is indulged in by the purveyors of what might be called 'tabloid religion'. Many churches now have regular healing services and one might detect a wide variety of motives and expectations in this. Obviously, what has been said about the miracles of Jesus and about miracles in general can be said again. There is much happening which cannot be explained and which might well come within the general ideas outlined earlier. The important thing is that it is neither dismissed out of hand nor made the basis of exaggerated claims. We believe that God is at work in and through the church; therefore we may well expect that on occasions the high points in the relationship, to which I have referred, will manifest themselves in extraordinary ways.

On the negative side, there is no doubt that miracles are big business in the hyped up world of media religion. As we watch some of the high-profile demonstrations which go on, it is worth remembering that Jesus' miracles, whatever else they were, were never crowd-pulling stunts; even though the crowds were undoubtedly pulled, that was not his purpose. That was one of the temptations he specifically rejected in the desert and the church would do well to follow his lead if it is not to become indistinguishable from a fairground. Indeed, it is worth pointing out that, where the crowds were drawn to Jesus by his miracles, he accused them of being impossible to satisfy.

> When the crowds were increasing, he began to say, 'This generation is an evil generation; it asks for a sign, but no sign will be given to it except the sign of Jonah. For just as Jonah became a sign to the people of Nineveh, so the Son of Man will be to this generation. The queen of the South will rise at the judgment with the people of this generation and condemn them, because she came from the ends of the earth to listen to the wisdom of Solomon, and see, something greater than Solomon is here! The people of Nineveh will rise up at the judgment with this generation and condemn it, because they repented at the proclamation of Jonah, and see, something greater than Jonah is here!'[58]

I recall a conversation with a colleague, about a church's obsession with signs and wonders, in which he said, 'I couldn't be minister of that church. Just think of the pressure – having to pull a bigger rabbit out of a hat every Sunday morning!' The insatiability of the people of Jesus' day is far from unknown in present day society or the present day church. Certainly, there have been some extraordinary things done in these kinds of religious gatherings. That simply means what it says – that things have happened which cannot easily be explained. It is a long way from there to a miracle. Equally, the mere fact that we find the concept of miracle more difficult than in previous generations should not close our

[58] Luke 11:29-32

minds to the possibility of events which are, if I may again use John Macquarrie's telling phrase, 'the approach and self-disclosure of [God] to us in, with and through the focusing event, bringing grace or revelation or judgment, as the case may be.'[59]

The fundamental question which I would ask about any claimed miracle is whether it is a sign of the kingdom of God. In asking that, I would wish to bear in mind the biblical accounts of the temptations of Christ and the suggestions put to him then. Is the context of the claimed miracle more akin to the sensitive, acutely personal ministry of Jesus, or does it more readily make us think of someone jumping from a steeple to draw the crowds? This is the key to the whole issue. In the example I cited at the beginning of this chapter, there was no public spectacle. It might well be that, at the time, only I and the people directly involved were aware of it – and perhaps only one of them. The only reason it was spoken of openly was that the subject of continuing the 'Hand in Hand evenings' was under discussion; the term 'miracle' was never used, and there was never a moment's suggestion that it had any propaganda value. However, it was certainly seen as a moment of disclosure, a sign of the kingdom: it was 'the approach and self-disclosure of [God] to us in, with and through the focusing event.'[60] It was *seen as* a miracle.

This seems to me to indicate a direction of thought which is likely to be fruitful. Miracles, then, are a sign of the efficacious involvement of God within creation: high points in the relationship, moments when creation is responding to God's constant involvement in such a way that extraordinary things happen. They are not arbitrary interventions which suspend the action of nature. From this position we are ready to move on to consider the other part of the equation, which is prayer.

[59] John Macquarrie: *Principles of Christian Theology* (SCM 1986) p.252
[60] John Macquarrie: *Principles of Christian Theology* (SCM 1986) p.252

What is the Point of Prayer?

It seems a good question: if God is always and actively involved in creation, and if he is not going to intervene specifically on our behalf even if we ask him, then what is the point of prayer? It is a depressing fact that many people seem to regard prayer almost as a switch which can be thrown to activate God when necessary. Perhaps we should ask: do we only speak to our friends and family when we want something from them? We might find our spiritual lives a great deal less arid if we did God the courtesy of speaking to him the way we (sometimes!) speak to others. Whilst we shall not have the scope here for an exhaustive treatment, it may be helpful to take a brief look at the subject of prayer.

Many people struggle with the stereotyped concepts of prayer, and I have often found it necessary to try to introduce a broader understanding. While the traditional approaches are important, there are also ways of actively relating to God which may not have the outward appearance of 'prayer'. We may be reading the newspaper or playing with our children, but the spirit in which it is done may bring it into the realm of prayer. More of that later, but let us look fairly briefly at some traditional forms of prayer with which we are perhaps most familiar, and see how they can be understood in terms of a relational God.

Prayer as Relating

As soon as that heading is used, then it reminds us that we are praying not to an interventionist but to a relational God; not to a God who *intervenes*, but a God who is *involved*. That being so, there is clearly little point in praying in order to persuade, but every point in praying simply in order to relate. Prayer is the expression of a relationship. If our prayers are dominated by requests, then we must ask what is lacking in our relationship with God.

It is not difficult to see that prayer is much more than merely 'talking to God', let alone presenting a shopping list.

We can readily appreciate that it must involve listening, but it needs to go far beyond that. There is a story of a priest who noticed an old tramp in his church. The man was there often, on weekdays, and seemed simply to sit for long periods of time. He never attempted to beg from the clergy or other visitors; he was there in good weather as well as bad which meant that he probably was not merely sheltering there – at least in the simple sense of the word. After a while, the priest felt it appropriate to ask the obvious question and, following the usual 'Good morning,' he asked the tramp if he would mind explaining what he found so attractive about the church. He received a devastatingly simple answer: 'I look at him, he looks at me and we're happy together.' Most of us know people with whom it is good simply to spend time, without having constantly to do or say things to justify it. Why, then, do so many people – including this author – find contemplative prayer so difficult? I do not propose to embark upon a treatment of that subject here; there is an abundance of books available by much better qualified writers.[61] I simply wish to bring the subject within our frame of reference to indicate that prayer is really about spending time consciously with God. That time may be used in a variety of ways, but simple stillness is a vital part of it.

I remember a woman who was associated with a church where I served. Her day began early and finished late, and she was simply always on the go. Her whole life was devoted to her family, but it was not difficult to sense that there were other reasons for her throwing herself into constant activity. One day she said to me, 'I suppose you're going to tell me I ought to pray.' My response was that she certainly needed some space to be still. Since she was always up well before anyone else, would it bring the family's life to a halt if she spent the first few minutes of the day simply sitting quietly? In a day which began and ended when most people were in bed, it was tragically clear that there was no room for a few

[61] See, for example, Merton, Leech and Hughes in the Bibliography

minutes' quietness. We may call it prayer or something else, but God calls us to stillness because he recognises it as a very real need; and in my work as a mental health chaplain I see many examples of the destructive effects of hyperactivity and the legacy of the 'Protestant Work Ethic'.

Adoration and Praise

It is easy to be baffled by the idea that God actually *wants* or even *asks for* our praise. If God counts humility as a high virtue, then it is hard to imagine him as basking in praise. Furthermore, it seems actually somewhat presumptuous, even patronising, for mortals to tell God how great he is. What is really happening, though, is that we are celebrating the greatness of God – enjoying being in his company. Again, as with our other relationships, sometimes it seems appropriate simply to be quiet together and at other times we throw our dignity to the winds and have a knees up. Both of these, and the many intermediate stages, are appropriate at different times. However, we are not doing it to massage God's ego but to enjoy his presence. The celebration feeds the relationship, enables a different kind of communication, puts us in touch (if it is communal worship) with a wider circle of friends of God and increases our commitment to keep up the relationship when the dryer times come.

Confession

Now here is a hot potato! The whole concept of confession has been seriously abused in Christian circles – and not only in the Roman Catholic tradition. We need carefully to consider the place which this particular activity has within our relationship with God. In all traditions, particular insights have led to practices some of which are healthy and others distinctly unhealthy. The practice of confession in front of another person, for example, is not confined to the Roman Catholic church and its positive value was recognised by no less a Protestant than Dietrich Bonhoeffer himself.[62] He recognised the positive value both of unburdening oneself in another's presence and also of hearing through that other person God's assurance of pardon. He made the point that it is one thing to know with our minds that God has forgiven us, but quite another actually to hear the words with our physical ears. At the same time, he made it clear that this was a *mutual* activity, and specifically warned against the practice of one person serving as confessor for a whole community. In this, he carefully avoided endorsing the traditional idea of the confessional uncritically.

What, then, is the true purpose and value of confession in the context of a relationship with God? Surely, it is about unburdening ourselves onto the God who always longs to forgive – not about simply rehearsing lists of supposed wrongs to the extent that we end up feeling worse than before! We all have things in our lives of which we are not particularly proud but about which nothing is now to be done. Confession enables us to face up honestly to those things, recognise them for what they are, and be assured that they need not be forever a burden to us. It is also about facing those things which can be changed and being assured that the grace to do so is available to us. So it is a positive experience.

Confession may take the conventional form, or it may not. If we believe in a relational God who is in all things, then simply talking about our regrets, our fears, our hang-ups with another person and hearing them respond positively may also be a way of communing with God who is in that person and in the relationship we have with them. Once again, though, it would be important not to wallow in our sense of guilt but to accept the assurances that are offered and then leave the issues behind. The vital point is that confession is not a way of flogging ourselves or of manipulating God, but is his means of liberating us for something ultimately more useful.

[62] Dietrich Bonhoeffer: *Life Together* (SCM 1985, ch.V)

I would regard this kind of practice as sacramental in the true sense of the word. In the non-judgmental listening and acceptance of another person, and in the assurance of forgiveness which we are able physically to hear, we have an 'outward and visible sign' of an 'inward and spiritual grace'. For those whose sacramental sense is more specifically defined, the pronouncing of absolution by a priest is not by any means to be denigrated. The important thing is that the person receives the assurance of forgiveness which is needed, and if they find it easier to accept that from a priest then that is where they should go. However, whatever form of confession is used, we should be aware of the dangers. There is no doubt that a very unhealthy dependence can be created, and this is the case whether the confessor is a priest or not. This is why Bonhoeffer stressed the mutuality of confession. I believe he has a very valid point, since that mutuality is a partial safeguard against at least one form of abuse. I know a number of cases of people who have been encouraged to talk openly in prayer meetings about very personal things, 'so that we can pray for you'. There is no doubt that sometimes this is handled well and is a source of healing. However, such groups must always be on their guard against allowing the practice to become a cover for less noble motives, and it is unfortunately clear that in some cases it has been little if any better than a licence for prying. Prayer circles which offer this very valuable help must therefore be aware of the issues of confidentiality which it raises, and the potential minefields to which it can lead. My own personal belief is that it should never be undertaken without careful training; working in the sensitive area of mental health has heightened my awareness of what a complex issue confidentiality is, and the very difficult position in which it can place those who undertake the role of confessor. Having flagged up those warnings, however, I repeat that when handled sensitively, in a genuine atmosphere of mutual trust, it can be a most beneficial form of prayer.

For most of us, I imagine, confession will more often be a private activity; a regular part of daily devotions. Here it serves a vital function in allowing us to face those things which we would never articulate in the presence of even the most trusted friend or partner, not necessarily because they are more shameful or embarrassing than others but simply because there are things which are special to us; ours and nobody else's. In the privacy and intimacy of private prayer, they can be faced and the wounds exposed for healing. Again, though, healing is the objective and not an increase in guilt. If any form of confession leaves us feeling worse than when we started then we need to ask questions and perhaps seek advice. The purpose of confession is to find assurance of forgiveness and to be released from burdensome guilt.

This subject raises other vitally important questions about the whole subject of repentance and forgiveness, which I shall attempt to open up in the next chapter, in considering the subject of atonement.

Intercession and Petition

This is the most problematic form of prayer, for it is generally understood as a request for God to intervene. However, is it not vitally important in a healthy relationship that we share our concerns with one another even if we do not expect any specific action from the other party? Do we not even say things which the other knows perfectly well, simply as part of the sharing process? Of course God does not need us to tell him that the Kurdish community in Iraq is suffering terribly, but we may still feel it important to express our concern about it. When we pray for our relatives and friends, almost 'routinely', it could be said that that too is quite unnecessary as we already know that God cares for them. Again, we only need to look at our day to day personal relationships to see the shallowness of that assertion. When my wife and I used sometimes to take our son over to spend a few days with his grandparents, we would often say utterly silly things like, 'Look after him, won't you?' I say 'silly', because there was no possibility that he would be entertained in anything less than a royal style! Yet they were not offended by what we said;

they knew that we trusted them and those words were just our way of expressing our love for our son. In a similar way we pray for our loved ones, in effect saying to God, 'Look after them, won't you?' It does not imply lack of trust; neither is it an attempt to persuade God to do anything which would not have been done anyway. It is simply our way of letting God in on our lives and our loves. If someone tells me they are praying for me, I generally respond very warmly, not because I think God is going to do something as a result of their reminding him which otherwise he might have overlooked, but because it is good to know that they care enough to include me in their prayers. Surely, it is right that we should share with God our hopes and anxieties, our pride and our concern about those we most love.

Principally, though, intercessory prayer is a way of opening ourselves up to God in order that we can participate in his hopes and dreams for creation. While we certainly should not expect to twist God's arm through prayer, it may be that God will twist ours a little – or at least prod our consciences. While we are praying for the lonely person down the road, God might just put it into our head that we should get off our knees, onto our bike and go and pay the person a visit! I remember hearing a sermon in which the minister cautioned us against glibly asking God to show us what to do, since God might well take us up on it! God's response to intercession can be demanding for us. There is a story of a Korean priest in prison for his faith who saw another prisoner shivering, asleep on the cold stone floor, and he found himself asking the question, 'If that were Christ, would I give him my blanket?' So as a result of the priest's prayerful openness to God, his fellow prisoner was a little warmer – at some considerable cost to the priest. Perhaps one reason why we tend to cling to a more simplistic concept of prayer is the hope that we might retain our own blankets. This story leads on to another aspect of prayer which is often not even considered.

'Sanctified thought'

During a discussion at theological college, I commented that I believed it was possible to pray through reading *The Guardian*. One of the tutors teasingly enquired whether I could do the same with *The Daily Telegraph*. Humour aside, the point of the conversation was again the nature of intercessory prayer. What I was saying was that God opened me up to issues in new ways through a variety of means. If we are reading about, for example, the policy of the United States toward Cambodia, and if we are doing so with an awareness that God is in that situation and calling us to respond, then I believe that such an activity is prayer – defined as relating. We should expect to find God speaking to us through drama, literature, television, sport, any medium at all. Indeed, such is the greatness and the humility of God that we might even hear the still small voice while watching an imported soap opera!

That last example may, in fact, make the point very well. During a period of convalescence, I found myself watching some of the more undemanding television programmes. One particular soap opera began to hold my attention, not because the storylines were anything special but because I got involved with the characters. Two in particular, a married couple, had a kind of gruesome fascination as their marriage began to fall apart. The reason for the break-up was that they simply were not communicating. For all the shortcomings of the storyline, and the inadequacies of the acting, the writer actually did a very good job in highlighting their predicament. Each of them was blinkered by stereotyped ideas, unreasonable expectations and a complete inability to dismount from the high horse and really communicate. Is it fanciful to think that God spoke to me and, more to the point, that he might also speak to a few people with similar relational problems, through what must honestly be described as very poor drama?

Genuine openness to the creation in which God is involved must surely open us to God, and allow new insights to be put before us. If that spurs us to some sort of action, then our prayer will have changed something.

Prayerful relating

Another interesting memory from theological college: we were asked to go into groups and discuss – as far as we felt able – issues which were of concern to us, finishing off the session with prayer. It so happened that in our group was a student with a very particular concern which occupied a great deal of the time. The group as a whole was very open and sympathetic and listened carefully to what was said, people occasionally asking questions which indicated that they had understood and/or wished to understand better. The person who had become the focus of the group's attention said afterwards how helpful the session had been. One member, however, was becoming more and more agitated as the time went on, and repeatedly said, 'We must stop or we shan't have time to pray.' Others in the group were convinced that the whole time had indeed been 'prayerful' as we allowed the relational God to move in our relationships and shed light on some very sensitive questions. Now, during the half of each week I spend as a mental health chaplain, I am frequently asked to pray with people. Even if I know the person extremely well, I never pray without first listening. Most of the time is spent in conversation, and only after that process has begun to have its effect is a formal prayer introduced. Once again, if we believe in a God who works in and through relationship we should be able to recognise this as a perfectly valid form of prayer in itself. So our formal prayers do not need to be overlong if we are prepared to give to God the listening and the thoughts from which they spring.

God is in all creation, and in all people. Prayer is relating to God, and whenever we relate genuinely and openly to others and to the created order, we can be said to be at prayer in some sense or other.

In the course of this chapter, as might have been expected, it has been necessary to rethink the concept of miracle somewhat and to give some careful consideration to the question of prayer. I make no pretence of having produced a comprehensive review of the subjects; rather, the aim has been to show how we may continue to value them while allowing our understanding of God to grow. The key, once again, is the concept of God as relational. Both miracles and prayer are expressions of creative relationship, as well as the means of pursuing it, and when seen in that way it is perfectly reasonable to believe in both.

CHAPTER SIX

Atonement

In Christ God was reconciling the world to himself[63]

To apply the word 'crucial' to this particular area of faith is more than just an apt pun. Having apparently left behind the idea of a God who intervenes in favour of a God who is in constant involvement, working through relationship, we now come face to face with the intervention to end all interventions. At the very heart of the Christian faith stands the cross, and the claim of Christian tradition is that God intervened in human history in a unique way. Now once again we could take a giant leap to the position of regarding the cross as purely symbolic. I say 'purely' because there is no doubt that the cross *is* symbolic, but that does not mean that something real was not also happening there. However, I shall suggest that the cross can be seen as the supreme act of a *relational* God: a God who gets involved.

This is a key area of theology which has been under continuous discussion from the earliest days of the church. That discussion has produced a variety of ideas and schools of thought, some of which are extremely helpful while others are decidedly less so. However, it would be neither possible nor helpful in this book to rehearse the debates of twenty centuries; if readers wish to pursue those arguments there is no shortage of excellent books to help[64], but that is not my purpose here. Rather, I hope to show how the doctrine of atonement through the cross is of central importance to the concept of a relational God, as that is understood in Christian tradition.

[63] 2 Cor. 5:19

[64] cf. Paul S Fiddes: *Past Event and Present Salvation* (DLT 1989), and *The Creative Suffering of God* (OUP 1989) but see also the Bibliography at the end of this book.

That tradition makes a number of significant claims about the death of Jesus:

- Jesus died for the sins of the whole world.
- At Calvary, Jesus came under the judgment of God.
- His death was a sacrifice with atoning power,
  by which we are saved.

At the beginning of this discussion, let it be clear that I believe all of this. The important thing to remember is the respective roles of the 'cart' and the 'horse'. The statements made above were ways of expressing the mysterious reality which the followers of Jesus experienced. Unfortunately, they have since been taken to be the *starting points* for theology, with the result that, in cultures far removed from that in which those statements were helpful, some rather strange things have been said about God. But that is what tends to happen when one tries to explain explanations!

What I propose to do, in so far as I am able, is to place the horse once more in front of the cart: to begin by trying to understand a little of what the passion of Jesus can tell us in terms of God's dealings with humanity. Then it will be seen that those early explanations do in fact make sense, without the need to construct theories of the atonement which Jesus might have found at best incomprehensible and at worst thoroughly offensive.

From the beginning, I have been arguing for a relational concept of God. This means trying to understand the cross both in terms of God's action and our response. If we ignore the former, then we make it all dependent upon ourselves, which is a matter for despair if past indications are anything to go by. If, on the other hand, we completely neglect the aspect of the human response, then we are back to the *God in control* model which is unacceptable. So I propose from the outset to think in terms of relationship.

Theology finds itself apparently on the horns of a dilemma. On the one hand, the frequently expressed idea that Christ in some way stood in for us and was punished in our place raises questions about the nature of God. What sort of God punishes the innocent in order to pardon the guilty? If it is said that the demands of justice had to be met then are we saying that God is under the law? Analogies with the law court run into serious difficulties since, obviously, a human judge is under the law which is made by a superior institution. God, of course, is subject to no superiors. On the other hand, if we reject this idea, are we in danger of failing to take seriously the enormity of sin, with its horrific and often uncontrollable consequences? We must on no account do that, and this writer is among the last to do so, but we need to make an effort to understand the process of atonement in ways which do not do violence to the nature of God.

In order to do this, we must look at the all-important matter of context. I believe that some of the less helpful explanations of the cross have arisen from the well-intentioned attempt to apply in our own setting images and ideas which are really only fully comprehensible in the quite distinctive culture of Judaism with its rich and powerful traditions. I therefore propose not to embark upon an exegesis of the crucifixion narratives, but rather to consider the key themes of judgment and sacrifice, and the related issue of forgiveness and repentance.

JUDGMENT

Eternal Hope[65]

Can the Father in his justice burn in everlasting
flame
souls that, sunk in foulest squalor, never knew
the Father's name?

Can the love of man be greater than eternal
love divine?

[65] G. A. Studdert Kennedy: *Rhymes* (Hodder and Stoughton 1932)

Can the heart of God be harder than this
hardened heart of mine?

Can the pangs of hell be endless, void of object,
void of gain,
save to pay for years of sorrow with eternity of
pain?

Cursed be the foul contortion that hath turned
his love to hate,
that hath cried at death's dim portal, 'Enter
here, and 'tis too late.'

Cruel pride and vain presumptions claim to
grasp where angels grope;
'tis not God but mean man's blindness dims
the deathless star of hope.

Geoffrey Studdert Kennedy was an army chaplain in the first World War, who became famous as 'Woodbine Willie'. His poem is powerful stuff, wrought of many years' exposure to painful suffering in other people, both in war and in 'peace'. However, what he would not do – as we shall see later – is use this kind of thinking to cheapen the atonement experience. We must do justice to the seriousness of sin, and therefore the consequences of it, without at the same time attributing to God characteristics which would make Hitler look like a boy scout. We shall begin by examining one of the best known parables of Jesus.

The parable known as the Prodigal Son, but which has more aptly been called the 'Waiting Father',[66] is a parable of judgment and atonement. I propose to use this as a point of reference in considering those aspects of God's relationship with creation. However, one thing must be absolutely clear:

[66] Luke 15:11-end

this parable is about God's relationship with creation. It is emphatically not, in its original sense, about the relationship between the first and second Persons of the Trinity. I make this point because too often the classical doctrine that Jesus 'carried our sins' on the cross has been interpreted in a way which divides the Trinity, setting the Father against the Son. It is just an unfortunate coincidence that this parable is about a 'father' and a 'son': the father, of course is an image of the God of Israel, not the Trinitarian 'God the Father', and the son is an image of fallen creation.[67]

As the parable begins, the son – who is legally old enough to be responsible for his own affairs – asks for the means to pursue an independent life. What is the father's response to be? He could refuse on the grounds that his son is too immature and will almost certainly make a mess of it. He could also refuse on the grounds that when the son gets into trouble it will be the father who will have to rescue him. Or he could consent, with the disclaimer, 'Don't come running to me when you're in trouble; you've made your bed and you can lie in it.' Finally, given that this father represents a loving God, he could say, 'Yes of course you can have the money, and if you ever get into difficulties I'll bale you out.'

Significantly, the father in the story does none of those things. Apparently he simply gives the son his freedom and watches him leave, no doubt fully aware that he's headed for trouble.

The father has exercised a judgment. He has weighed the possible outcomes and decided that his son must be allowed his freedom; the freedom to reject his father's care and to go his own way. But there is also a more far-reaching judgment involved. The son's decision to strike out on his own will have consequences, and those consequences must be allowed to follow. I have pointed out before that freedom without consequences is illusory, and the offering of such freedom is patronising. So the father takes the risk of giving his son both

[67] However, for a creative use of this connection see Henri J. M. Nouwen: *The Return of the Prodigal Son* (DLT 1994) p.55ff.

freedom and the means to exercise it. This is not a matter of weakly 'giving in'. The father has weighed the issues discussed in earlier chapters of this book, concerning freedom and consequences, and has decided upon his course of action. He has used his 'judgment'.

We may now see the subsequent misery of the son as the product of two things: his own foolishness and his father's 'judgment'. In a very real sense, when he wallows in the pigsty he is suffering under his father's judgment. His father has judged that he should be allowed true freedom, which means the freedom to do things which bring bad consequences. Now, were I to suggest that his father had actively wished that such a fate befall his son, it would be patent nonsense. Such a monstrous attitude would be quite incompatible with the father who is portrayed at the end of the story. Yet it is too often considered quite acceptable – even necessary – to believe in a God who inflicts pain and suffering as a punishment precisely for the sin of wishing to live our own lives. Of course, what God actually does is respect our freedom, which means respecting also the consequences of our decisions. However, we must say more than that if we are to do God anything like justice.

There is a missing element in this story – missing precisely because it is a parable, in which the central point must be reached with the minimum distraction. But we may allow ourselves a little more latitude. If this were a play or a novel, we should be complaining about lack of detail. To be specific, what is happening 'back at the ranch' while the son is bringing about his own downfall? Is life going on as normal with no thought for the lost son? Clearly not, if the context of the story is taken seriously. The lost coin and the lost sheep are searched for until they are found. The attitude portrayed there must certainly apply in this parable, since they are all about God, but the father cannot so readily search for his son, who is capable of free and informed decision, without compromising his freedom. However, the clue is nonetheless there if we read carefully. The father sees his returning son from a long way away, and has clearly been on the rooftop looking for him. At the first sign of his son's return, he is rushing out to meet him, not waiting for the carefully rehearsed apology but joyfully and spontaneously offering reconciliation.

In the light of the cross event we can now see the missing element in the parable. The problem for the son, far from home, is that he has no way of knowing what his reception will be like. Perhaps the pigsty is preferable to a triumphant or patronising reception from the parent, not to mention what he will get from his safe, steady, even good, but mind-numbingly dull older brother! Certainly, countless young people sleeping rough in our cities will testify to that feeling. And a further problem for us in interpreting the parable is that it makes God distant and uninvolved. It has been observed that a God who does nothing is in some ways more contemptible than a God who loses his temper. However, the Christian doctrine of incarnation rescues this parable from incompleteness. God has made the journey into the far country; he has taken up residence in the pigsty. In the cross event, he has shown that he will sink to the lowest possible depths: wherever people are in the dung, however deeply immersed, he will go and be there with them. And he will stay with them for as long as it takes. Now the prodigal has the opportunity for reconciliation, for the presence of his father in the pigsty does two things: it presents the son with the awesome nature of his sin in inflicting pain and degradation not only upon himself but upon his father; and it assures him that there will be no recriminations. He may safely return to his father's house and, while he might still want to make the apology he has rehearsed, he will do so out of genuine remorse and not for what he might gain by it.

The Christian claim is that, in Jesus, God made the journey into the far country; shared its joys as well as its pains with us, and stayed with us through the worst possible experiences that we can face. In short, God has opened the way for atonement (at-one-ment). Of course, to do full justice to this we must change the tense, and say that all this is still happening. God repeatedly and constantly makes that journey, sits in the pigsty and by his suffering presence moves the human heart to repentance and salvation.

Having said that, however, we are by no means finished with the parable, for there is yet another very telling image of judgment in it. We are presented with the elder brother, clearly much more deserving of his father's affection than was his junior sibling. He, it appears, is not pleased by the reconciliation which has taken place. We may well say that he is all too representative of the society we know which is far more anxious to see 'sinners' punished than to share the joy of heaven in their repentance. I well remember the furore when a convicted murderer, having served his sentence and satisfied all the relevant authorities that his repentance, conversion and calling were genuine, was accepted for ordination into the priesthood. Another classic example would be the harsh judgmentalism generally directed at those who succumb to any kind of sexual temptation. (It is strange how congregations where the ninth commandment[68] is constantly broken through 'harmless' gossip become terribly moral when someone is believed to have transgressed the seventh!) Self-righteous judgmentalism and a desire to see 'sinners' get their 'just deserts' might give us some sort of short-lived satisfaction but it cuts us fellow sinners off from the joys of real relationships. In the parable of Jesus, we see how the thoroughly deserving brother of the 'prodigal' *excludes himself* from the celebrations. The father, in fact, begs him to come in but he refuses. He has not been rejected by his father, but has just as firmly shut himself out by his own pride and jealousy. The image, then, is of the father longing for reconciliation but having to accept that, just as the younger son was free to 'do his own thing', so too is the elder. Another 'judgment' has been made, and this time it is the apparently righteous elder brother who is living under it.

[68] Exodus 20:16

Here we have an image of judgment which is entirely consistent with the cross. The pain of humanity and the pain of God are one (but not *one and the same*).

This idea must not be used to proclaim what Dietrich Bonhoeffer called 'cheap grace', which fails to take seriously the catastrophe of sin and the cost of reconciliation. The judgment of God brings us face to face with the enormity of sin, and this happens supremely in the cross. A very healthy view of judgment, which also avoids the danger of cheapening grace, is found in another of Geoffrey Studdert Kennedy's poems.

Judgment[69]

There is mercy with thee,
therefore shalt thou be feared.

I saw no thronged angelic court, I saw no great white throne,
I saw no open judgment books, I seemed to stand alone.
I seemed to stand alone beside a solemn sounding sea,
while at my feet upon the shore broke waves of memory.
Their murmuring music sobbed, and sought a way into my soul,
the perfect past was present there, and I could see it whole,
its beauty and its ugliness, its sorrow and its sin,
its splendour and its sordidness, as wave on wave rolled in.
And ever deeper pierced the pain of all that I had lost,

[69] G. A. Studdert Kennedy, *Rhymes* (Hodder and Stoughton, 1932)

my dear dead dreams of perfect things, I saw them tempest tossed.
They fell like wreckage at my feet, and as I turned them o'er,
the solemn waves, in Memory's caves, kept booming, 'Nevermore!'
There came one dream, more dear than all, a corpse without a head,
the flying spray hissed cowardice, and it was dead, cold dead.
Then suddenly a shadow fell, and I was not alone,
He stood with me beside the sea, and listened to its moan.
I did not dare to raise my eyes, I feared what I might see,
a cold sweat broke and bathed my brow, I longed to turn and flee,
but could not; rooted there I stood, in shiv'ring shame and fear,
the subtle shadow substance took, and nearer came, and near.
O was it days or was it years, we stood beside that sea,
or was it aeons, timeless times? It seemed eternity.
At last, compelled, I raised my eyes. Two eyes looked into mine,
and shattered all my soul with shame, so sad and so divine.
It palsied all my pride with pain, the terror of those tears,
and wrought into my soul the woe of all my wasted years.

'Depart from me,' I cried, 'depart, I cannot stand with thee
and face the sorrow of those eyes beside this cruel sea.
Depart from me, I dare not tread the sands those feet have trod,
nor look into those eyes that tell the agony of God.
Depart,' I cried, and he was gone. I stood there all alone,
in silence save that memory's sea still made perpetual moan.
Night shadowed all, and wandering winds came wailing from afar,
but out across the darkening sea shone forth one single star.

Here, Studdert Kennedy portrays no instant transformation from guilt to innocence, from pain to bliss, which would simply not take the lives we live here seriously. Rather, we are shown a facing of reality. The 'wasted years' matter, and they cause God pain. The wasted or deliberately avoided opportunities to be there for others, to relieve pain, to enable growth, to promote wholeness, all those are tragedies for ourselves and for those we have failed, and God cannot simply say the failures are unimportant without saying the *people* we failed are unimportant. So the judgment is that those failures and disappointments must be faced. The presence of Christ is painful not because there is a moment's reproach, but because of the 'sorrow of those eyes'. The 'judgment' of God is that for at-one-ment to take place we must be involved in that sorrow, even if it hurts like hell (I choose my words advisedly). However, the real nature of God – and the real purpose of judgment – shows at the end of the poem. Ever humble, ever respectful of our freedom, Christ departs when he is so bidden; but not without leaving a sign of hope: just the light of a single star; enough to keep hope alive and to invite us to go forward, but not enough to overrule our choice.

The sins of the Parents

The biblical writers understood God's judgment well when they said that the sins of the parents are visited on the children for several generations. That idea gives us a further insight into the seriousness of sin for people designed for relationship. It also helps us to understand how the sins of earlier generations have caused the whole of humanity to be alienated from God to such an extent that drastic action was necessary. To unpack that, it would be helpful to return to the parable of the prodigal son, and take the liberty of extending it somewhat further.

Let us suppose for a moment that the son never found the courage to go home, but remained in the far country. Suppose he was able at some time to marry, most probably someone in a similarly desperate state to his own, and they had children. We now have a generation who have never known any other condition than that into which they are born. Life in the pigsty is 'natural' and, while they may not like it much, they do not see the possibility of anything else. In time, they start to learn about their grandfather, who appears as rather a remote figure. Apparently, he lives in splendid isolation while his family are in squalor, and since Dad is afraid of him then the children will be so, too. The sense of alienation is compounded, and increasingly so as the later generations follow. When the son dies, his children and grandchildren remain alienated. They may themselves be absolutely innocent, but they are estranged from their grandfather just as if they had been guilty. The sins of the parent have truly been visited upon the children, and will be for many generations. They are suffering as a result of the quite proper 'judgment' of the grandfather (for our purposes we shall ignore the fact that he is now an incredible age!) who knows that freedom means that actions must have consequences – even when they affect the innocent. The more time passes the more futile it all becomes, and clearly the grandfather cannot allow this to continue if he is to be able to live with himself. If he is truly loving, then he must find a way – he cannot simply be satisfied with academic theories when his family are suffering so. There is only one thing to be done. He must make the journey into the far country, sit in the squalor with his grandchildren and build from scratch a completely new relationship with them, based on personal knowledge and not on the distorted impression they have gained from their errant father.

Of course, we are in danger of stretching the parable beyond reason, and our use of it must end there. Far-fetched though it has become, however, it makes the point. We are all victims of the sins of past generations, and the more time passes the more trapped and alienated we are. Because we are made for relationship, the consequences of the actions of the guilty often fall upon the innocent.

Clearly, then, we must be very careful how we talk about judgment. It is clear that we all suffer under the judgment of God, because of what we may (in a loose sense) call 'original sin', but that is a long way from claiming that the judgment is deserved. We may be paying the price of our forebears' follies, but we are not 'being punished' for them. The gospel – the 'Good News' – is not about sin and judgment, but about love and forgiveness. The Good News is precisely that, in Jesus, God has made the journey into the far country. He has sat in the pigsty and let his family experience for themselves what he is really like. He has shown that there is nothing of which to be afraid. And to make that crystal clear, when the family turned upon him in fear and anger, he took all the pain and allowed himself to be trampled in the dung before offering a whole new life and a whole new relationship.

The Cross as Judgment

Now it becomes clear how we may say that the crucified Christ suffered under the judgment of God. Jesus, our tradition says, was sinless and yet he suffered because of the sin around him. He became the victim of the prejudice, anger, pride, greed and so on of his contemporaries, and the judgment of God is that the consequences of those sins must be allowed to work out even when it affects innocent people. This judgment was accepted by Christ in perfect obedience. However, we must bear in mind what has been said already: if God was 'in Christ', then this was no easy, detached, academic judgment. Rather it was a profoundly costly one for God since it meant being utterly immersed in the pain which it involved. The 'father' was in the pigsty. Even that, however, is not enough. This event must have some saving power. The presence of God in the pigsty is only of value if it has the power to bring about change in the relationship and restore hope to a lost creation. The way into that issue is via the other vital element in atonement.

Sacrifice

In discussing sacrifice, it is worth pointing out that in the Old Testament, sacrifice which was merely ritual or which was claimed to have some quasi magical effect was consistently denounced as meaningless. Sacrifice was a way of representing in ritualistic form what was a daily reality in terms of people's relationship with God in their lives. Therefore, it would be equally wrong to regard Christ's sacrifice as simply a ritual with some sort of quasi magical effect. Just as the sacrifices that we offer must be related to, symbolic of, illustrative of the lives we lead in relation to God, so the converse must be true of the sacrifice God offers for us.

Sacrifice is often talked about as if it were purely a biblical concept, and as though it only had one meaning. Frances Young[70] dispels both those myths, pointing out not only the variety of meanings which sacrifice conveyed to the Hebrew people but also the widespread use of it in other cultures. The primitive idea of sacrifice as a bribe designed to place God, or

[70] Frances Young: *Sacrifice and the Death of Christ* (SCM 1983)

the gods, under an obligation, or as a way of 'feeding the gods', is clearly untenable if one is committed to a relational view of God. Further, the very idea that God can be obligated to respond to our initiatives is clearly nothing short of heretical.

The second understanding of sacrifice, as a way of appeasing God's anger, seems to me to be only slightly, if at all, different from the first. The only difference is that, while the first approach was designed to oblige God to intervene, the second is apparently intended to oblige him not to do so; not to inflict punishment. The emphasis is different but the principle is the same; God is being manipulated by human rituals to behave in ways which we desire.

A better understanding of sacrifice, especially for Christians, is the *communion offering*. Not only in Hebrew, but in Greco-Roman culture, the practice developed of eating the sacrificial animal at a communal meal where the god was believed to preside. We can immediately see the relevance of this idea not only to the Christian eucharist but to the very concept of a relational God to which this book is committed. It is a communal activity in which God and people share; a mutual self-offering but with God very definitely recognised as the initiator.

Also prevalent in the ancient world was what Young designates *aversion sacrifices,* in which whole animal corpses were burnt or buried in order to ward off evil. Various theories about the Christian understanding of atonement have been built around this idea, Satan either being frightened off by the sacrifice or being tricked into thinking he had won, only to have victory snatched away at the very last moment, leaving him trapped and doomed. This latter idea, of course, is open to the serious objection that it presents God as defeating the devil by sinking to the same level of deceit and underhandedness. If we believe that in the cross evil was overcome by good, then we cannot accept this interpretation.

When aversion sacrifice is used to represent the Christian idea of atonement, it seems that a very primitive understanding of sacrifice has, so to speak, skipped a generation, for such an idea was quite foreign to the biblical world of the Hebrew people. For them, the burning of a whole carcass in this way was seen as an act of thanksgiving, rather than a warding off of evil spirits. The concept of God among the theologians of ancient Israel was much more developed than we often seem to realise.

The Blood of the Lamb

The early Hebrew people were aware of a very basic fact of life which we have touched upon already. They knew that, because we live in community – in relationships – the actions or omissions of one person can affect many others. They became aware that the effects of sin had a pernicious and disastrous way of spreading. A dispute between two people could soon engulf their families, their neighbours, innocent passers-by, and could rapidly undermine the peace and harmony of a community. In our own history, we have learnt that the abuse of power by an employer or a trades union can breed resentment, distrust, create industrial chaos and bring down a government. Just as surely, racial or cultural pride in an apparently insignificant non-commissioned officer can combine with the hurts and grievances of others in such a way as to lead to world conflict and the decimation of an ethnic group.

For a more recent example, we may cast our minds back to the Gulf war. While recognising that there were some very complex issues involved which are outside our field, we might see some significance in the way the issue was handled. What began as a dispute between two states (and one in which the rights and wrongs were nothing like so clear-cut as they were claimed to be) the dispute became, in all but name, a world war as alliances were formed (human rights records of, for example, Saudi Arabia being conveniently forgotten in that cause) and individuals and families well removed from the situation were drawn in at great cost to themselves. Most significantly, a powerless and already oppressed group (the

Kurds) became pawns in the hands of the great powers involved, were drawn into the conflict by false hopes of liberation and finished up being punished by the Iraqi government and ignored by the Allies. Thus we could say that the self-interest of a few power-hungry people – not only in Iraq – spread and infected whole communities and nations to engulf innocent people who had done nothing to deserve their fate. In one way or another, the whole world was contaminated by an evil of quite localised origin.

The Old Testament people understood this danger better than we appear to know it. So they developed rituals for dealing with the malignancy of sin and preventing its spread. They needed a disinfectant and, in the absence of Imperial Chemical Industries, turned to a more organic source. Since it was said that the spread of sin caused death, what better antidote than the substance which was believed to contain life? So it was that the blood of a pure creature became associated with the renewal of life after the fatal contamination of sin.

This can be illustrated well by reference to the often-used word, *expiation* which simply means 'covering'. We have various examples of this in our own situation, upon which we may draw. When a person dies, the body (if not cremated) is buried, and in hot countries this happens very quickly indeed. It is usually done, of course, in a dignified manner which serves also as an important ritual element in the grieving process; but the fundamental reason why the body is buried is to prevent the spread of infection. For similar reasons, we sometimes cover unpleasant substances if it is not possible entirely to clear them away, in order to render them safe while the natural degradation process goes on. So the early Hebrew community, recognising that the infection of sin could not easily be removed, began to think in terms of 'covering' it. Again, the best thing with which to cover sin, which caused death, was something which contained life.

We can see from this the significance of the use of blood, and also the importance of the purity of the creature from which it was obtained. However, there is a further dimension to consider: that of cost.

Dealing with sin is costly. Sin cannot simply be shovelled into a dustbin, or covered over with some soil. Like a major ecological disaster, such as the explosion at Chernobyl or the firing of the Kuwaiti oil fields, it offers no quick fix, no cheap solution. So it was necessary to avoid giving the impression that some quick easy ritual could deal with the tragic consequences of sin. This was accomplished, to some extent, in the requirement to offer not only a pure animal, but the best in the flock. In an agrarian community, living under precarious conditions and without the sheer abundance which modern factory farming allows, the giving up of the best lamb in the flock was a serious business. And let us note that the preferred animal was a lamb – not a sheep which might by now have paid for itself in terms of producing lambs or wool – but the very best of the prospects for the future. This is costly indeed!

In the offering of a perfect lamb as a sacrifice, then, the early community sought to express the awesome seriousness of sin, and the incalculable cost of dealing with it. The difficulty was, of course, that the sacrifice could possibly express something of that, but it could not actually deal with the sin. The awareness gradually came that it would need some pretty spectacular intervention by God to deal with a contamination of this scale. But how can a relational God intervene, without compromising the free relationship? Both for God and for us, the search for that answer leads to the cross.

The cross shows us how the 'germs' of sin multiply, and sin spreads. The 'ordinary', 'little' sins which we daily excuse in ourselves (though less readily in others) of jealousy, resentment, pride and so on – sins which we too often lightly describe as 'only human' – these are the sins which crucified Christ, and not some dreadful, extraordinary cosmic evil. Those very familiar failings of humanity eventually become so out of control that whole groups and nations are infected and the innocent suffer.

At Gethsemane, Jesus faced the result of that process and was presented with two possible alternative responses. He could add to it or he could absorb it. One of his disciples, in trying to stop the evil, actually added to it when he unsheathed his sword and attacked the High Priest's servant[71]. Jesus pointed out that that was not the right way of dealing with the situation. Instead, he not only offered no resistance but actually healed the wounds of one of his oppressors[72]. He met evil with good. We might perhaps speculate as to the likely outcome had Jesus decided to meet force with force. The result, undoubtedly, would have been that a lot of people would have been hurt, and perhaps killed. In the volatile atmosphere of occupied Jerusalem at Passover, the spiral of revenge and retribution which that could have unleashed hardly bears thinking about. By his refusal to use violence, Jesus did two things. Firstly, he prevented the sin from spreading. He 'covered' it and saved the community from being infected and perhaps destroyed by it. Secondly, he accepted the *cost* of that kind of love, and in doing so willingly participated in God's costly work of redemption. Christ made himself a 'sacrifice'.

Sacrifice is a particularly helpful way of thinking about atonement since we know that it is essential to any relationship. Any friendship, any marriage, any creative interaction between people involves a process of self-limitation. Our time, our desires, our ambitions, our personal space may well have to be limited or even put at risk. Most importantly, our desire to be in control must be replaced by an openness to mutual exchange which depends just as much on the other party as it does upon us. The mutuality of sacrifice forms the basis of the relationship. Earlier, I was suggesting that we need to think in terms of God's limiting himself in order to allow true relationship to grow. Here we see Christ limiting himself in his response to the evil around

[71] Matt. 26:51 par.
[72] Luke 22:51

him in order to keep open – or to reopen – the possibility of relationship.

I have argued right from the beginning that God has chosen to involve creation in a partnership. Therefore we must make reference to the responsive sacrifice which all who would enter this relationship must make. It will now be readily understood that this is not because God arbitrarily demands it, or because he takes some kind of pleasure in our discomfort. It is because, as has been made clear, any relationship involves sacrifice. In a television programme about marriage, which was about as superficial as most such programmes are, one person who was interviewed said he kept away from all relationships 'because they involve sacrifice'. He was to be given credit, of course, for being perceptive enough to understand that; how sad that he was not also perceptive enough to realise how much he was denying himself. If we are to enjoy any kind of relationship then we must make the sacrifices in terms of individual freedom which it involves.

So our responsive sacrifice, in seeking a relationship with God in Christ, is actually a participation in the sacrifice he makes. We, too, will find our scope for doing as we please curtailed. Of course, we shall not find God as unreliable a partner as he finds us to be, but since our relationship with him is expressed in relationships with each other, we shall certainly be open to the same kind of abuse. We, too, shall find that those whom we love do not always love us back; that some of those to whom we offer ourselves take what they can get and give nothing in return, and so forth. In our way of handling all that, we too shall sometimes be called as Jesus was to stand under the judgment of God and suffer undeserved pain at the hands of those we love the most; we shall also be called to react in ways which prevent the evil from spreading by meeting it with good. Some people have found that that even involved the shedding of their blood and the sacrificing of their lives. Dare we say that their blood has become associated with the 'blood of the Lamb'?

We have far from exhausted this very fecund image of sacrifice, but hopefully the essential groundwork has been done to enable further thinking. The important thing is that sacrifice is not something God demands in order to appease his anger; rather it is something God offers, at enormous cost, to overcome the catastrophic effects of sin and keep the mutual relationship open.

Now it would be useful to return to the statements I made at the beginning of this chapter, and see whether those classic claims can be upheld by what I have proposed.

- We may say that Jesus died for the sins of the whole world since we recognise that the sins which crucified him, far from being the inhuman excesses of a few extraordinary people, were in fact the ordinary 'little' sins which we too often excuse as 'only human': anger, jealousy, resentment, fear of people who are different, selfishness – all the 'little' flaws in human nature which we recognise and excuse. If we need it spelled out more clearly, let us imagine the reaction of many Christian churches today if Jesus introduced into the congregations the kind of people whose company he actively sought and encouraged in first century Palestine! Jesus was a threat to the *status quo* and he died at the hands of respectable, devout religious people and pillars of society. Had we been there, it is not hard (but it is very uncomfortable) to work out on whose side we should probably have been! Yes, Jesus died for the sins of the whole world.

- We have already seen how we can say that Jesus came under the judgment of God, as the consequences of those very ordinary sins were permitted to work out, despite the fact that the victim was innocent. By the way he died, Jesus accepted that judgment.

- We have also seen how the term 'sacrifice' can very accurately and helpfully be applied to the cross. The cost of redemption is that of holding open a relationship come what may; of offering love and forgiveness in the face of monumental evil; of refusing to add to the evil there already is. I recall a television programme, at the height of the troubles in Northern Ireland, in which Roy Hattersley was asked, 'Why should we treat the IRA any differently from the way they treat their victims?' His simple but devastatingly telling response was, 'Because we claim to be better than they are.' Evil cannot be defeated by a more powerful evil – that merely adds to it and exacerbates the consequences. But to meet evil with good, violence with non-violence, hatred with love, imposes a cost; it demands a sacrifice. That is the sacrifice Christ made.

The question remains as to how that sacrifice could have atoning power for us now. Again, there are many possible ways of attempting to answer that question, but I shall confine myself to two points.

Firstly, because of the cross of Christ we all know the immense seriousness of sin in the way 'little failings' mount up to become something much more than the sum of the parts. This realisation can move us to repentance and genuine renewal of life. And the image of a suffering God also breaks through the barrier of fear and enables us to return to God, since one who will undergo such pain and humiliation for our sake is not going to punish us. Like Geoffrey Studdert Kennedy, however, we shall certainly not escape the bitter pain of facing up to our failings.

Secondly, we recognise the cross not only as an historical event but as an ever-present reality. At the heart of all the suffering which our abuse of our freedom creates we see a still-crucified God, showing us the enormity of our sinfulness and lovingly calling us to repentance with the same assurance of pardon and reconciliation.

This sort of view is often dismissed as 'mere psychology', to which I would reply in two ways. Firstly, as I have argued before, God presumably understands psychology better than any of us and it seems reasonable that he, as the greatest psychologist, should use it. When it is used in this kind of way there is certainly nothing 'mere' about it; indeed, I should describe it as highly sacramental as the 'outward and visible sign' opens us up to receive in copious measure the 'inward and spiritual grace'. As such it also holds together the objective and subjective aspects of atonement, in terms of God's initiative and our response. Secondly, if the term 'mere psychology' suggests that I have not covered the whole subject, then of course I agree that I have not.

I stated at the beginning of the chapter that I did not propose to offer a complete treatment of the subject of atonement, and I have certainly not done so. However, I hope I have shown how the traditional statements about the death of Jesus can be made and used in ways which are healthy and helpful, and which open up the possibility of a growing relationship with the God revealed in Christ. If so, then I hope to have provided a starting point and indicated a possible direction for the continued exploration of the mystery of the cross. I can do no more than that; the reader must make the journey. Yet it would be wrong to leave the subject of atonement without considering another issue which is very much in need of careful consideration both within and beyond the Christian community.

Forgiveness and repentance

Over many centuries, and certainly in recent times, both of these notions have been cheapened and thereby brought into disrepute. In modern usage, forgiveness is all too often represented as a kind of 'That's all right, don't worry about it,' following an equally superficial token apology. It is also used to encourage the suppressing of feelings until they turn in upon their subject and seriously damage mental, spiritual and physical health. Similarly, repentance is often portrayed as little if anything more than a verbal apology, which empties it of all value. Worse, it turns what should be a positive opportunity for change into a convenient sandpit in which heads can be buried. It enables the culprit to avoid facing the seriousness of the offence, and puts the person offended against under psychological pressure to say, 'That's all right,' even if it is not meant; and so the cycle continues.

As a minister, I had to lead a family service on the subject of forgiveness, and in order to do so I 'set up' some incidents which were to happen during the service – having of course forewarned the congregation to expect the unexpected and not be alarmed when it happened. One member of the congregation was holding a tambourine, having used it in a previous song, and another was holding an old and now broken watch which despite its worthlessness looked quite impressive. I began a stereotype 'sermon' and, after a few minutes, the tambourine was noisily dropped. The worshipper made great play of retrieving the instrument and profusely apologising to me. I made equally great play of smiling benignly and assuring him that I did not mind in the least, before straightening my face and adding in a stage whisper, 'Stupid idiot!' The children loved it, while the adults were distinctly uncomfortable! A few moments later (again by secret prior arrangement) I broke off the sermon to launch a verbal assault on another worshipper, complaining that her 'bored' expression was putting me off. She replied, as per our agreed 'script', that the sermon was boring, and I had only myself to blame, upon which I demanded an apology. (The children, by now, were clearly thoroughly enjoying the spectacle and finding it anything but boring!) When I made it clear that I was prepared to hold up the service until I received the apology, it was given, with very dramatic ill will!

Finally, a few moments later, the watch was dropped and 'broken', the culprit then expressing profuse apologies which I airily and benevolently dismissed with, 'It doesn't matter.' The sham sermon was then abandoned, and we discussed the three incidents.

Clearly, in the first example, the apology might very well have been real but the 'forgiveness' certainly was not. A number of people commented that they had been rather less offended by my insulting remark than by the sheer hypocrisy. To say that we forgive somebody is meaningless unless it is real. At best, the forgiveness was a misguided attempt at 'niceness' which did not deal with the reality of the feelings; at worst it was a blatant lie, intended simply to get the incident out of the way so that I could continue to enjoy the sound of my own voice. Either way, it was certainly not real forgiveness.

The second incident was flawed both in terms of forgiveness and of repentance. The apology, having been forced, was given grudgingly and with poor grace. The acceptance of the apology – with a magnanimous assurance of forgiveness – was patronising and insulting. Furthermore, not only had the relationship not been healed; it had actually been made worse. The way the apology was elicited had turned what might otherwise have been a momentary lapse in an otherwise good relationship into a more lasting breach which might, were it real, have taken years to heal if it ever did.

The third incident illustrated what is in some ways the most dangerous misuse of this concept. During the reflection upon it, I introduced a new (fictional) element into the drama by telling the congregation that that watch was far from unimportant. It had, I said, been my mother's last gift to me and as such was of inestimable value and quite irreplaceable. But in order to keep the relationship superficially sweet I had told the person who dropped it that it did not matter. I, of course, would then have had to live not only with the breakage of that precious article but with the feeling that by denying its real value I had dishonoured the memory of the person who gave it to me. There could be far reaching consequences both for my own personality and for my relationship with the other player in the drama who, of course, would be unaware of the underlying causes of those problems.

Before proceeding any further we did something which, incidentally, is of paramount importance if this sort of role-play is ever used: we 'de-roled'. Each of us stated that it had been fictional, and that our relationships were (as was indeed the case) extremely good. The human personality is a complex and delicate organism, and that procedure must always be followed after any kind of unscripted role play, especially if it has involved confrontation and hostility.

So, what did we learn from all that? Forgiveness and repentance are not some mechanism by which cracks are papered over. Such a misuse is very much worse than doing nothing at all. Doing nothing at all would leave a gaping wound for everyone to see which might well be offensive but would at least be visible. This kind of conventional politeness, however, conceals the wound and leaves it to fester at the same time as adding the further contamination of hypocrisy and self-reproach. Entire communities of Christian people are debilitated by this 'gospel of niceness'[73] and their whole life and mission are subverted.

It is of absolutely paramount importance that we learn ways of being honest without being offensive. We really must be able to trust what fellow Christians say to us, especially in this most sensitive and fundamental area. No apology should ever be given unless it is utterly genuine and heartfelt. Similarly no words of 'forgiveness' should ever be used unless they are meant. This will mean we shall have to abandon the easy options of speaking in traditional clichés and find other forms of expression. It may well be that the best an offended person is able to say is, 'Our relationship cannot be as it was, at the moment.' It may or may not be honest to add the hope

[73] *cf.* Alastair V. Cambell: *The Gospel of Anger* (SPCK 1986)

of a future improvement, but that also should be withheld if it is not genuine. Similarly, the person who caused the offence might be able to say nothing more than, 'I honestly don't think I did anything wrong, but I am sad that you have felt hurt.' In the third of our role-play situations, it might have been considerate not to tell the culprit the full significance of the watch, but it could have been possible to say, 'Actually, it did have a lot of value to me, but I value your friendship and wouldn't want this to come between us,' if the latter part were true.

Forgiveness and repentance are really about the restoring of relationships which allow everyone involved to grow both as an individual and as a member of the relationship. This is more likely to happen through honesty than by superficial expressions of feelings which are not genuine.

Repentance and Forgiveness: Chicken and Egg

The commonly accepted belief is that repentance is required before forgiveness can happen. While aware that it is not a simple question, I believe the Bible generally tends to emphasise the priority of forgiveness, or at least the offer of it. We can cite innumerable passages from the Bible which show God taking the initiative in atonement, and actually going to find the lost. If we read the stories of Jesus, we find that the offer of forgiveness seems to precede any show of repentance, or indeed to happen without any such expression at all. To the man who comes in through the roof, he simply offers forgiveness and scandalises his hearers in so doing. Supremely, of course, he prays for people who not only are not repenting but are actually carrying out the most ghastly attack upon him as he says the words. Where, then, do we find the idea that repentance must precede forgiveness? The answer is, of course, we find the idea in the Bible, and too often for it to be dismissed as a mere accident. Forgiveness depends, in some way or other, upon repentance. and yet we also wish to say that, since the love of God is unconditional, then the offer of forgiveness must be so too. How can we say that?

We must return to the point that forgiveness is about the setting right of a relationship. If we remember also that relationships which are of any value at all must be freely entered into on both sides, then the mist begins to clear a little. As with the chicken and the egg, we may find it difficult to know which comes first but we do know that they are mutually dependent on one another. Anyone who has ever tried to offer an apology to someone who will not accept it knows very well how impossible reconciliation then is. Similarly, though, there can be no real reconciliation between two parties if forgiveness, when offered, is not accepted in a proper spirit. So it is perfectly reasonable to say that repentance is necessary for forgiveness to be effective, in the same way that any gift (which forgiveness is) cannot be forced upon someone who will not accept it. Having said that, it must be firmly stated that God's *offer* of forgiveness is unconditional. It is we, not God, who make the acceptance of it, and the completion of the reconciliation so difficult. As Studdert Kennedy observed, earlier:

> 'tis not God but mean man's blindness dims
> the deathless star of hope.

CHAPTER SEVEN

RESURRECTION

Christian faith is *resurrection* faith. From whatever theological position we approach it, all Christian faith ultimately centres upon the resurrection. Our concern is with how it affects our lives here and now. How does the relationship with God which we call faith respond to the belief in resurrection? Ultimately, it is that question which matters much more than any other. As with so many aspects of faith, we find that the meaning of the event is more important than the mechanics.

Having said that, it would be helpful to outline some of the basic arguments if only to show that those who are committed to the traditional belief have good reasoning to offer in defence of it while those who take a more questioning line are far from being without faith.

The questions which have caused so much more heat than light over recent years are not new, but have been around for hundreds of years; indeed, we only have to read Paul's letters to find that questions about the nature of Jesus' resurrection predate the writing of the gospel accounts. Before going into some of the issues, perhaps it would be best to begin by making a few statements on which the overwhelming majority of theologians from both sides of the argument agree.

- Jesus died by crucifixion at the hands of the Roman authorities. This is attested both by the records kept by the Romans and by contemporary Jewish historians. There have been suggestions that, unknown to the authorities, Jesus was not really dead but had fainted, later to recover and emerge from the tomb. Although it has in the past been advanced by some highly respected thinkers, I find this suggestion very difficult to take seriously. Not only is the likelihood of the Romans making such an error remote in the extreme, but the conditions inside a sealed tomb would hardly have been conducive to recovery after such a trauma as crucifixion. That Jesus, in the condition in which he would have been, would have had any prospect of breaking the seals and moving the stone with his bare hands seems to me highly optimistic – and if he had, then the pathetic spectacle he presented would hardly have inspired awesome worship in his followers. I believe we can safely accept the testimony of scripture, of historians and of official chroniclers: Jesus died on the cross.

– While we may hold differing views about the details, we would also agree that *something happened* in the succeeding days or weeks which had the effect of turning that demoralised, frightened group of disciples into courageous public figures ready to die for the cause of Jesus. Some are only prepared to say that it was a psychological process which led to this, but even that is to say that something happened. And, once again, presumably God knows all about psychology and could have been in that process. Others will say very firmly that what happened was precisely as described in scripture: that Jesus was raised physically back to life on the Sunday, and the tomb discovered inexplicably empty. Yet others will say that Jesus was indeed raised to life, but it was not the same body. More of this shortly.

- Whatever it was that happened on that first Easter morning, it was something of momentous, life-changing importance. In other words, it had an *effect.* We are not involved merely in some dry historical debate, and the important question at the end of the day is about what *effect* this mysterious event now has upon us.

That last is the point to which we shall be returning later, and which will be the real point of this chapter. First, let us briefly look at some of the issues. We begin by making a key distinction between two words which are frequently confused.

RESURRECTION OR RESUSCITATION?

Bishop David Jenkins hit the headlines of the more sensationalist press when he used the memorable phrase 'conjuring tricks with bones'. He was reported as having likened the resurrection to such a stunt. In point of fact, the precise opposite was the case; he was *contrasting* rather than *comparing* the two. He was trying, as always, to expand our vision and help us see the faith we hold in much fuller ways. That the media were able to make so much hay while this particular sun shone – and that it shone for so long – is an indication of how unclear our thinking is on the subject of resurrection.

Jesus was not the first person recorded in the Bible to have been raised from the dead. Both in the Old Testament and in the gospel narratives before the crucifixion, we can find stories of dead people being raised to life. As soon as that assertion is made it should become obvious that, if we are to continue to see Christ as 'the first fruits of those who have died'[74], then we must ask what distinguishes his resurrection

[74] 1 Cor 15:20

from these other apparent examples. One has only to sit in one of all too many churches around Easter time, when the story of Lazarus comes round in the cycle of readings, to hear the distinction being blurred if not lost altogether. The 'simple' answer is that what happened to Jesus was resurrection, whereas all the others are examples of resuscitation. Corpses were brought back to life. To say that is not for a moment to deny the momentous significance of the events, but to describe *resurrection* in those terms would be rightly offensive. That is why Jenkins was always careful to say that the resurrection of Jesus was *infinitely more* than that.

The easiest way to distinguish the two phenomena is to ask a question. What happened to Lazarus, to Jairus's daughter and to the others who were resuscitated? They came back to their old lives, exactly as they had been before, and at some future date presumably they died. I say 'presumably' because it is of course not made explicit, which in itself suggests that the life they lived after the event is not of world-changing significance to us. It is the event itself which is important.

Very well, then; let us now ask the same question about Jesus. The answer, we find, is dramatically different. The picture we are given here is of radically different new life, gloriously free from all the constraints which the structures of this world had attempted to impose, and – most importantly – a life for which there would be no more death. This is why Paul can use the telling phrase I quoted earlier: first fruits indeed! This is not simply a replay of what has happened before, but something entirely new. The promise is not 'more of the same' but is of infinite possibilities never before dreamt of. We might say that this is a matter not of 'coming back from the dead' (as Lazarus did) but of going forward *through* death as tradition says only Jesus could do.

This kind of image of course must not be pushed too far or we end up by pushing Christ himself out of this world. The point is that the promise we claim to hold is one of new life, always leading us forward to infinite possibility.

Why believe in a bodily resurrection?

The most obvious reason is that that is what the Bible says, and that argument needs to be taken seriously for one does not need to be a biblical literalist to adopt it. Many serious scholars have concluded that the biblical evidence is so strong, the nature of the accounts so convincing and the context of the event so extraordinary that the basic story must be accepted.[75] They make a very weighty argument, but the question is far from closed. The stories of course were written some years after the event by which time there is no doubt that the belief in a bodily resurrection had taken hold in the church. So vivid was the experience, and the conviction of the disciples, that it could only be described in that way because human language is severely limited. Some historians would question whether there would ever have been any question of the body being buried in a tomb in the first place, the more common practice being incineration in the constantly smouldering valley of Gehenna (the word often used to denote hell in the New Testament). Again, though, it can be argued that Pilate, having blotted his copy book very badly on other issues, might have been willing to make concessions on this point for the sake of a quiet life. Altogether it is an extraordinary story and so the unexpected can hardly be ruled out in this of all cases!

A line of argument which does seem to me to be impossible to sustain is that the resurrection was God's way of providing *irrefutable proof* of Jesus' divine status. This argument is frequently used manipulatively, to curtail discussion and discourage further exploration. Yet the story as we have it in scripture seems itself to suggest that the resurrection was never used as proof in the forensic sense of that word, and never could be. In the four gospel accounts there is not one single mention of a witness to the resurrection itself. One of them tells of an earthquake which frightened the life out of

[75] See, for example, John Polkinghorne: *Science and Christian Belief* (SPCK 1994) ch. 6

the guards, but all they saw was an angel coming from heaven and opening the tomb. In the other narratives, there is not even this concession. The tomb is mysteriously open, as it would be if it had been robbed. In a purely scientific sense, the evidence simply is not conclusive; indeed, I strongly suspect that were a religious cult today to present identical evidence for the claimed resurrection of their leader, the response of the Christian community would be sceptical in the extreme! Clearly, therefore, there is no question of the resurrection *proving* anything, in the sense in which that word is generally used. Once again, the neurotic demand for a 'sign' is refused and we are called to take the risk of faith.

This of course is absolutely consistent with the way God works. Nothing is done to compel belief, or to make a particular response inevitable. From a perspective of faith, the evidence God offers us opens up new possibilities of understanding, but the evidence is always refutable. This is the only way God can respect our freedom. All that is required for faith – for relationship with God – is there if we seek it, but for those who are minded to refuse the relationship, there is always the scope to do so. Here we may remember that the stories of resurrection appearances are all to people who had been with Jesus in his ministry; that is, to people of faith – people whose faith had crumbled under pressure, certainly, but people of faith, however frail, nonetheless. The nearest to an exception to that is the 'appearance' on the road to Damascus to someone who was fairly clearly on the brink of conversion before the event happened[76]. Had God been trying to prove something, I am confident it would have been proved and not left with so many loopholes which people committed to the Christian faith (let alone those opposed to it) are able to find. The resurrection certainly offers a confirmation of faith – and for 'those who

[76] The sheer ferocity of Saul's persecution of the church suggests that he was, even if unconsciously, going through processes of denial and projection which are now familiar to psychologists. This is reinforced by the words he says were addressed to him: 'It hurts you to kick against the goads.' (Acts 26:14)

have not seen'[77] a basis of faith – but not proof in the presently understood sense of that word.

The most convincing argument for a bodily resurrection is not an historical but a theological one. There is a case to be made for the belief that a bodily resurrection affirms God's commitment to the ordinary flesh and blood – the very stuff of our earthly existence – in a way which nothing else could. Surely, we believe in a God who is so committed; scripture and the better strands of Judaeo-Christian tradition bear witness to that faith. It can be argued that for God simply to ignore the body of Jesus and do something completely new would have been a denial of that; and this whole line of argument is reinforced if we consider the wounds in the risen body of Christ. Not of course that they *prove* anything to us at this distance from the event, but they do offer powerful imagery. The risen body of Christ is also the crucified body. This is wonderfully portrayed in Revelation, where the victorious Lion of Judah is the Lamb who was slain[78].There is continuity. The resurrection does not wipe out the past but completes it. As such it is consistent with God's way of working. The scars caused by sin have not been magically wiped away, but are still only too gruesomely evident. Here we have perhaps the crux of the issue (no pun intended) for we see the events of crucifixion and resurrection inextricably united in the broken body of Christ. However, there is also a warning here which the apparently confused imagery of Revelation highlights. There is continuity but not conformity. The Lamb becomes the Lion while still remaining recognisably the Lamb. Again we recall David Jenkins' famous warning not to reduce the resurrection to a conjuring trick with bones. The resurrection body bears the scars of pain, but is at the same time transformed and glorified. We may recall the extraordinary freedom of movement Jesus apparently enjoyed, unconstrained by bolts and

[77] John 20:29
[78] Revelation 5:5-6

bars[79] and apparently able to walk alongside long-standing friends for several miles without their recognising him[80]. This is a body which is not to be contained within any categories. The previous attempt to 'pin it down', so to speak, proved futile and we should not repeat the folly! All of which serves to lead us on to the next consideration.

Why believe in a purely spiritual resurrection?

We have already noted that truth and fact are not the same. A story may be positively bursting with truth while not being strictly factual, while another may be absolutely factual but convey nothing of significance. We have only to take a cursory look at the widely differing biblical accounts of the resurrection to know that they cannot be 'factual' in the strict sense. It is crystal clear that these stories were never intended to be regarded as factual evidence but as theological interpretation. That in itself does not of course rule out a bodily resurrection, but it means that we cannot use the biblical stories as hard evidence in its favour.

Again, there is a theological argument to be advanced. It can very fairly be said that the difference between the *resurrection* of Christ and the *resuscitation* of Lazarus, Jairus's daughter and the rest must be radical and profound and not just one of degree. This is an event utterly without precedent in human history. However, while being without precedent, it must also be – and this is the heart of the matter – the crucial event which brings history to a climax. According to the Christian claim, the death and resurrection of Christ make sense of the entire collection of beliefs, prophecies, hopes and expectations which form the Hebrew tradition. The past is fulfilled and the future anticipated in this event.

That, as Don Cupitt, points out, offers a very different understanding of resurrection. According to what he terms

[79] John 20:19
[80] Luke 24:15*ff*

the Theological Theory[81] (as distinct from the Event Theory) the disciples' first realisation of resurrection came as they reflected upon the events of Jesus' life and death and gradually saw the pattern emerge, recognising Jesus as that very fulfilment of history and promise. After all, Cupitt argues, if we accept the narratives which say that most of the disciples did not actually witness either the death or burial of Jesus, it seems unlikely that their immediate response on seeing him would have been to believe he had died and risen. A much more likely response would be that he had never really been killed: that the rumours of his death had been exaggerated. In order for them to grasp the significance of his resurrection appearances, they would have to have had their minds opened already. So Cupitt offers us the theory that it was theological reflection which made the disciples aware of the resurrection of Jesus and opened their minds to experience his risen presence. The stories of an actual tomb-bursting event developed as the gospel was proclaimed, but in the context of cosmic history the reality of resurrection is something infinitely more significant than the revival of a corpse. So the resurrection of Christ is clearly going to be a mould-breaking operation. It can no more be likened to any other raising of the dead than can the rising sun to the switching on of an electric light. Whatever superficial similarities there might be, the two events are of completely different orders.

However, Cupitt's Theological Theory, as he articulated it in that book, is not the same as saying that the resurrection was 'all in the mind'. What Cupitt was saying in this particular instance was that the disciples' awareness of the resurrection required a sounder basis than seeing someone whom they believed (but probably did not *know*) to be dead, up and about again. There may or may not have been an empty tomb, and the actual body of Jesus may or may not have been raised, but faith cannot be said to depend on either of those.

[81] Don Cupitt: *Christ and the Hiddenness of God* (SCM 1985) pp.164*ff*

Against Cupitt, it has been argued that surely the disciples must have known that Jesus was really dead. The reports of witnesses, whether sympathetic or otherwise, would have spread rapidly and they would have no room for doubt. However, I am not at all convinced that this refutes Cupitt's case. The first stage of grief is denial, and this is especially so where the death has not been witnessed at first hand. I think back to my own response to a sudden and traumatic bereavement: I did not witness the death, neither did I see the body for some days. He was alive when I last saw him and a few hours later I was told that he was dead. The denial stage of the grieving process is something I remember vividly, and I am quite sure that, had someone told me just a few days later that he had been seen alive and well, my first thought would not have been of resurrection. It would simply have confirmed what part of me had believed all along: he had not really been dead; or it had been a mix-up, and someone else had taken my child when theirs died; or . . . All kinds of irrational ideas had supported the denial and few of them make any sense now, but at the time they would have made more sense than resurrection. So I do not think that Cupitt's 'Theological Theory' is anything like so easily refuted as the proposed objection would suggest.

From a somewhat different theological standpoint, Hans Kung also asserts that neither an empty tomb nor a resuscitated corpse should be the basis for resurrection faith. He points out that the earliest accounts of resurrection – found not in the gospels but in the letters – base their claims not upon an empty tomb but upon appearances of the risen Christ[82].

> It was not by the empty tomb, but by the 'appearances' or 'revelations' – probably subjective visions or hearings, in any case calls to proclamation akin to those of the prophets – that Jesus's disciples came to believe in his resurrection to eternal life.[83]

[82] cf. 1 Corinthians 15:1-8
[83] Hans Kung: *Eternal Life?* (Collins 1984) p.130

Lest the word 'subjective' should go unnoticed, Kung goes on to make the point more emphatically:

> The reanimation of a corpse is not a precondition for rising to eternal life. Hence for Paul too (and for the rest of the New Testament letters) what is decisive is not the empty tomb, which he does not mention at all, but the proof of Jesus as a living person. Christian faith therefore appeals not to the empty tomb but to the encounter with the living Christ himself: 'Why look among the dead for someone who is alive?'[84]

That this was indeed the case for the early disciples is borne out by scripture. The stories about the empty tomb were generally dismissed as 'old wives' tales' by the men; and whatever may be said about 'Doubting Thomas' he was far from alone in needing that real encounter before he could believe. The gospel makes clear that his problem was not lack of faith; it was his absence from the scene when the others received their first revelation. Uncomfortable as it may be, the biblical evidence is that few if any of the disciples believed on the basis of the empty tomb, but only following that vital encounter. Furthermore, even this was not enough for some, according to Matthew's account.

> Now the eleven disciples went to Galilee, to the mountain to which Jesus had directed them. When they saw him, they worshipped him; but some doubted.[85]

What, though, of the theological argument referred to earlier, about the resurrection as a sign of God's commitment to the whole person? Hans Kung again addresses this point.

[84] Hans Kung: *Eternal Life?* (Collins 1984) p. 131
[85] Mat 28:16-17

> Is it then a *bodily resurrection*, a raising up of a man with his body? Yes and No. No, if we understand 'body' in physiological terms as the actual body, the 'corpse', the 'remains'. Yes, if 'body' is understood in the New Testament sense as 'soma', not so much physiologically as personally: as the identical personal reality, the same self with its entire history.'[86]

So we do not need a literal bodily resurrection for that powerful symbolic statement to be made. Indeed, this understanding actually achieves a better result. It is not simply the flesh and blood of the mortal body which God respects but the whole personal history, including the God-given relationships which characterised the earthly life.

Kung's general line of argument, then, gives us continuity with those first disciples and the early church. For us, too, argue though we may about the empty-or-otherwise tomb, in the end it is simply not what matters. What matters is an encounter with the risen and living Christ. Like the disciples, we shall only truly believe on the basis of that encounter.

However, we have not finished, for there is yet another possible line of enquiry to be pursued.

Was the resurrection all in the mind?

If one adopts the belief that God is purely (I do not say 'merely') a concept, then of course one has to explain the resurrection and its effects upon people in psychological terms. I have said that I do not believe we need to go to this extreme in order to escape the opposite one; that we can reject the crudely manipulative *God in control* without having to say, 'Anything else cannot be God.' We can believe in a God who is at work in creation, and that belief can certainly encompass an objectively real resurrection, either of physical or some other form.

[86] Hans Kung: *Eternal Life?* (Collins 1984) p.131

I stated at the beginning of the chapter that most of us can agree that *something happened* which transformed those dispirited, demoralised men and women into a world-changing movement of amazing courage and conviction. Many would argue that it had to be something objective – something with its origin (if not its expression) external to the disciples themselves. This is what Don Cupitt calls the 'Beaten-Men Argument'. In rejecting it, he rightly points out that there are many examples of 'Beaten Men' who have made extravagant claims about the continued life of their heroes in order to continue the struggle, just as there are other examples of leaders known and acknowledged to be dead, but who are legitimately claimed to be 'alive' in that their cause continues. Cupitt cites as example: the *Che lives* posters decorating many students' bedsit walls following the death of Che Guevara. The 'Beaten-Men' argument, he says, is not convincing.

> . . . it is precisely among the powerless that such beliefs begin. The Prime Minister does not need a poster saying *Che lives* to encourage him, so he does not put one up.[87]

There is much force in this argument, but I think there are obvious differences between the cases of Guevara and Jesus. The followers of Guevara never claimed that he was literally alive; his grave is not empty and everyone is aware that the language is symbolic. As regards the other 'Beaten-Men' whom Cupitt cites, they also cannot be described as truly comparable with the disciples. According to the stories, the followers of Jesus were not revolutionary firebrands whose leader had been killed and who were determined to carry on the struggle. Rather, they were people who had already proved their utter lack of all the necessary qualities, having deserted their leader when the chips were down and – in most

[87] Don Cupitt: *Christ and the Hiddenness of God* (SCM 1985) p.142

cases – not even sneaked along to witness his death or burial. Some elements in the gospel narratives even suggest that they had returned to their former occupation, evidently with little or no thought of continuing the struggle. Ruth Page also takes up the argument:

> Twenty years on, Che is not the cause he was in Britain in the 1960s – whatever other sociological factors have to be taken into account and whatever memories remain in Cuba or Bolivia. The spirit which drove Paul round the known world and persuaded Peter to eat Gentile meat, which the Corinthian church enjoyed in their undisciplined way and the Galatians nearly lost through a relapse into law, which has gone its way through the chequered history of the church and beyond, had and has, *at the very least,* a vivacity and durability which is striking.[88]

I share Page's inclination to believe that the resurrection was not 'all in the mind': that *something happened* which did not depend on the disciples' faith. As Hans Kung puts it, it was their faith that depended on the event, and not *vice versa.*[89]

In the end, the case is unprovable – which is no great surprise since I have been arguing from the start that the things of God are precisely that. That does not mean that we are excused from using our minds, but it does mean that in the end we have to 'step out in faith' without waiting for a watertight assurance.

To call oneself 'Christian', it seems to me, is to claim to be open to a life-transforming relationship with God; that is to be people of faith. According to the discussion of the subject of faith in Chapter 2, that should mean that we are ready to

[88] Ruth Page: *The Incarnation of Freedom and Love* (SCM 1991) p.85
[89] Hans Kung: *Eternal Life?* (Collins 1984) p.133

allow the resurrection to transform our lives without wanting absolute proof about it.

In the end, the only question which really matters is, as suggested earlier, about the *effect* which belief in resurrection – founded upon encounter with the risen Christ – actually has upon our lives. What does it mean to be people of resurrection faith? Whatever we think about the historical questions, can we find common ground here?

Resurrection Faith

A strong part of Christian belief in resurrection is that Christ was the 'First Fruits'; that the resurrection of Christ is our assurance of resurrection to eternal life. My concern, though, in this book is with what it means to be people of faith in the here and now. What effect does the resurrection of Jesus, and the promise it holds for us, have on the lives we live here? So I propose to leave the question of life after death largely alone and concentrate on the question of *eternal* (which is not the same thing as 'everlasting') life as we experience it here and now.

I have asserted that resurrection differs vitally from resuscitation in that it is a matter of going forward rather than back. To put it in another, and perhaps more intimidating way, it is about going *through* death rather than drawing back from it. This way of expressing it immediately suggests that there is no escapism here. Yet that is just how resurrection is sometimes used. Christians are wide open to the charge of escapism, and it has to be said that all too often there is an alarming degree of truth in it. I must honestly admit that I recognised this in myself when I was recovering from a heart attack. Faced with the awesome reality of my own mortality I had to acknowledge that I had not got the subject of death as neatly worked out as I had pretended. Some people who work in the hospice movement say that Christians frequently make the most difficult patients, for they have never faced up to their own mortality before. Moreover, they have never faced up to their doubts, either. The prospect of eternal life had been used to avoid facing the issues. Now of course there are also countless examples of Christians who have faced death with inspiring confidence and faith, and they simply emphasise the point that resurrection faith has infinitely more to offer than escapism; it can actually enable us to face painful realities. What a tragedy, then, that so often it is used to avoid them!

During the Cold War era when the threat of nuclear war was on most people's minds, it was frequently claimed that to be afraid of such an event revealed a lack of faith. God, it was asserted, simply would not allow it to happen. He had fixed the time for the end of the world, and humanity could not take that initiative from him. Either, then, God would step in and prevent it or he would allow it only in his own time, in which case there was nothing anyone could do about it anyway. This of course assumed that a nuclear war would be the end of everything, but it is surely not too much to believe that even out of that catastrophe God has the power to bring good. Millions of years might be needed for such a process, and the result would doubtless be very different from the present world, but it must be within God's power. What was really going on in this debate, of course, was a mass impersonation of ostriches. The belief in resurrection and eternal life gave people an excuse to evade their responsibilities which were to work, organise, protest, campaign and do all they possibly could to avert the threat of a holocaust. It was escapism on a grand scale.

Another aspect of this of course has been the abuse of resurrection 'faith' which led Marx to make his famous comment that religion was 'an opiate for the people'. In other words, it was a drug administered by the wealthy and powerful to the poor and powerless in order to keep them happy. They should not mind being poor in this world because they were going to be wealthy in the next! An even more sinister development of this is the explosion of sects and cults which focus their entire message upon life after death.

They flourish most in troubled places where the urge to escape is strongest, and week by week people pour in for their fix of fantasy. Their only desire is to escape for an hour or so from the dreadfulness of this life. One can hardly escape the feeling that their vulnerability is being cynically exploited by those who are turning religion into a thriving business. People are then made dependent, and encouraged in their escapism, rather than being strengthened and enabled to live amid the painful realities they have to face.

For all kinds of reasons, Christians easily become obsessed with the prospect of heaven and we sometimes hear the complaint that we are so heavenly minded that we're no earthly use. But since we believe in a God who is involved in creation here and now, then we must believe that the resurrection has power to transform not only the future but the present.

Escapism

Sometimes it does indeed seem as though resurrection faith is entirely about getting us out of this world to a better one. Some popular songs such as *This world is not my home* reflect a kind of popular escapism which has no justification in scripture. Jesus did not offer his disciples a quick transportation to the next world. Quite the contrary: he gave them a solemn commission to live and work in this one. This is made clear in the resurrection accounts of Matthew and Mark by the injunction to return to Galilee – the place of mission. It was also the place of misunderstanding (even by Jesus' own family), misrepresentation and rejection. The disciples were asked to go back into the painful places they had been before, but to do so in search of the risen Christ who had gone ahead of them. *There they would meet him.* We shall return to this point before closing this chapter.

Luke puts a somewhat different emphasis in his narrative. For him, the focus is Jerusalem. The two on the road to Emmaus, having met the risen Christ, return to Jerusalem to tell the good news and find, again, that Christ is ahead of them. There, in the company of the other disciples, they again meet Christ and witness his ascension; and the final injunction to them is to 'stay here in the city until you have been clothed with power from on high'.[90]

So although we are right to think in terms of going forward to new life, for now it is new life *within this world.* We do not need to wait until after death before we can enjoy God's promise of life in all its fullness. The call – the invitation – is to live in a world characterised and scarred by crucifixion, avoiding none of its pain, but to live triumphantly (*not* triumphalistically!) amid all that, in the light of resurrection faith.

The distinction between 'triumphant' and 'triumphalistic' is a vital one, and is graphically displayed at the crucifixion. Jesus 'triumphed' by refusing to return evil for evil; refusing to succumb to the temptation to vent his anger, his sense of betrayal. There was no, 'Just you wait, I'll show you!' Quite the contrary: there were words of forgiveness for the people who were directly causing the pain. In the battle for short-term advantage and power, there can be little doubt that Jesus lost; but in the cosmic confrontation between good and evil, Jesus was triumphant precisely because he refused to be dragged down to the same level as those who were torturing him – even though it meant dying in apparent disgrace and failure and allowing his oppressors to believe they had won. Compare that with a modern day worship song which enjoys enormous popularity, claiming that God will give to us the ground we claim (who is serving whom, one might ask) and that the church will rule throughout the world. Indeed, suffering triumphantly and living triumphalistically are two very different things.

We might well say, then, resurrection life is not about being transported out of this painful, precarious world but being enabled to live hopefully and trustingly – triumphantly – within it.

[90] Luke 24:49

However, the gospel is a wonderful treasure trove of paradox!

Nostalgia

There is a well known song, 'Carry me back to Old Virginny' in which a black slave longs to be returned to a beautiful place known long ago.The interesting thing, however, is that it is not a place of freedom, but of slavery: 'That's where I laboured so hard for ol' massa.' It seems that distance is lending more than a touch of enchantment to the view. It is understandable that a slave, transported far from home and ill treated, should express a longing to go back in the words of that well known song. I remember experiencing a similar sort of feeling. One of the various jobs I did after leaving school was as an office junior: a job which I studiously loathed, although the firm and the people with whom I worked were not to blame for that. I simply disliked office work with an intensity which I thought could not be surpassed. That was before I joined the Army. Now here was the mistake to end all mistakes: out of the frying pan and into the burning fiery furnace. It was clear that no matter how long we knew each other, the Army and I were not going to see eye to eye. How I longed to be back in the office, with those wonderful people, doing that fascinating work! Why, I could never have been so happy in my whole life as I was then. In retrospect, the whole experience took on a rosy glow not because it had been happy in the slightest but simply because anything – absolutely anything – would be preferable to the Army.

It is not a new instinct; the women who first met the risen Jesus certainly had it. According to Matthew, they 'took hold of his feet', which sounds like rather more than merely a gesture of worship. The glorious past had returned, and they were going to hang onto it! This feeling is confirmed in the Johannine account where Mary Magdalene is specifically cautioned not to hold onto the risen Christ. One can imagine her thinking, 'Now we can go back to the way things were.' It takes but little thought to realise the futility of giving way to such an impulse. We have observed that those who were raised back to their old life eventually faced the same death once more.

In pastoral work one all too frequently comes across people whose relationships are in difficulties and who want to get back to some previous blissful existence. The problem is that, even if they can do so, they will probably find that it was not as blissful as it now looks. There is a very strong likelihood that whatever brought about the present crisis will bring about another. When people are in relationship difficulties it is usually because of a failure to move forward – not back. Jesus had no intention of taking his disciples back to a previous time. Why should he want to do so? Would either he or they want to return to the life they had had before: misunderstood by friend and foe alike, considered to be mad by his own family[91], on the run from the state,[92] constantly having to bandy words with small-minded people who wanted to trip him up, being criticised for doing good and finally let down by the people he most loved; why on earth should he have wanted to go back to that! Furthermore, it would be impossible. The new, transformed life which he now enjoyed was not to be put back into an old wineskin from which it would simply burst out. Any attempt to return to the old life, having now glimpsed the new, would be futile.

THE LIFE OF THE WORLD TO COME

The disciples of Jesus were called to return to the world, in which the old life was still being lived, and to live their new life within it. They were to live in this world by the values of the next. The glimpse which they had had of the new post-resurrection order was to be a sign of hope and protest in the present.

A classic example of this is found in the Negro spirituals which, to our ears, sound dated and appear to reflect an

[91] Mark 3:21
[92] Mark 14:13

otherworldly piety. While the slave owners thought the songs were about a castle in the air, to other slaves they were songs of protest, because the hope of a future kingdom of justice and peace is, by its very existence, a howling protest against all that is unjust and violent in this world. So the resurrection life lived by Jesus and, in the power of his Spirit, by his disciples, was to be a powerful protest which would eventually undermine the unjust structures and bring them down.

No simple 'return to the old life' could ever achieve this; That would be a matter of going back and trying again, rather than doing something radically new. It would be like a wasp repeatedly attacking the same window pane in the futile belief that it might eventually break through. The resurrection of Jesus removes the glass and allows us through to something radically different; a whole new world of limitless possibility.

The themes of 'going' and 'coming back' are explored in John 14-16 in which we are given exciting glimpses of wonderful new possibilities which will be opened up by this process.

> Very truly, I tell you, the one who believes in me will also do the works that I do and, in fact, will do greater works than these, because I am going to the Father.[93]

However, doing the works Jesus did is fraught with danger, and the life of resurrection faith will not be characterised by unadulterated bliss.

> If the world hates you, be aware that it hated me before it hated you. If you belonged to the world, the world would love you as its own. Because you do not belong to the world, but I have chosen you out of the world – therefore

[93] John 14:12

> the world hates you. Remember the word that I said to you, 'Servants are not greater than their master.' If they persecuted me, they will persecute you; if they kept my word, they will keep yours also. But they will do all these things to you on account of my name, because they do not know him who sent me.[94]

This is powerful stuff. Living the new life in the old world will incur the displeasure of the latter. It can be avoided of course by simply continuing to live the old life; living by the old values which the world loves so that the world will love us too. This is a disturbing text for those who long nostalgically to go back to the 'good old days' when going to church was a mark of respectability; a sign of being among those the world loved as its own . . .

So the images of going back and going forward both have, in their different ways, something to say to us. We are not transported out of this life, and neither are we simply given an extra helping of it. We are given the promise of new, transformed life and invited to begin living it now!

This means that the new life is lived in constant confrontation, tension and often dangerous conflict; but for all that it is a life from which, once it is tasted, we would not readily return to the old.

Some friends of mine left this country in the late Eighties to live and work among the poor in El Salvador, at the height of the civil war. In due course, they returned to Britain for a holiday and it seemed reasonable to expect that they would be glad of the break. While they certainly enjoyed the relief from tension and the reunions with old friends, they were nonetheless far from happy. In Britain, the elevation of greed into a national virtue was well under way, and their return to this country brought them face to face with the hype and the tragedy of the Eighties' 'economic miracle'. The sham faith of

[94] John 15:18-21

individualism and the idol of competition had created an ethos which set people against one another rather than bringing them together. My friends' commitment to the poor had taken them into a very different life where, amid all the undeniable terror, there was a growth of solidarity, of community, of interdependence, and where the whole value system of the people among whom they lived was radically different. They had had a taste of resurrection life, and they did not find being 'carried back to Old Virginny' an unqualified blessing. They returned to El Salvador with real gladness because they were 'going back to Galilee', to seek the risen Christ among his still-crucified people, and the letters I receive from them tell me time and again that they find him there.

A subversive hope

After U. S. forces had been in action in the war in Europe, it was realised that young men who had known nothing else but a simple, and perhaps already lost, rural life had now been exposed to something very different. Most significantly of all, perhaps, young blacks, who had never been counted equal until they became equally entitled to die for their country, had glimpsed and indeed experienced things which had been kept well out of their reach before. Some of them had been stationed in Britain, and experienced life without colour segregation for the first time. They had had money in their pockets and the same freedoms as everyone else. The uncomfortable, and alarming fact was that the soldiers had seen life of a kind they had never known existed, and they were going to bring stories and images of that life back with them when they returned. The old social order was going to be severely tested and would certainly not survive unchanged. And this testing would be all the more dangerous because this new life was not merely a picture postcard image, but something which they had tasted and known, and which they had found to be preferable to the old life 'back at the ranch.'

The Christian church has has a similar experience. We have

experienced the life of the risen Christ, and because of that we proclaim that what we see around us here is not the whole story; that the 'joys' and 'blessings' of a commercialised, consumer-driven society are not the last word. Why do we say that? Because we have seen a body get up and walk about? No. Because we believe stories of an empty tomb? No. We believe it because, first and foremost, we have become caught up in the life of one who lived radically differently. The story of new life in Christ begins well before the resurrection; it begins with a man who not only preached the Sermon on the Mount but lived it out as well. In him, we have found a whole new way of relating to creation, a whole new set of values and priorities, a whole new way of measuring the quality of life. We have seen that, and we have seen the cost of it because the man who lived it died cruelly at the hands of a brutal social system. But then we say, 'He is risen!' And whatever we believe to be the historical background of that, we believe that the life this man lived goes on and the love he showed is not subservient to death but continues now and stands as a thundering protest against all that is unjust and life-denying in the world. We believe that the values and priorities which shaped his life are God given and that God honours those who live and die by them.

In Christ, we have seen someone live entirely for others and not for the accumulation of wealth, power or privilege; indeed we have seen him renounce all of those as being of no value by comparison with the life lived for others. We have seen him embracing the most detestable, most objectionable outcasts from society (going by society's standards, that is), and we have seen him building relationships of love and joy which nothing in life or death could destroy. We have seen *life!* How can we now return to the old life by assenting to the values of a mad, power-hungry, fundamentally unjust social order? The power of resurrection faith should make us as much a threat to all that is shameful in our own societies as were those returning soldiers who had 'seen the world'.

The Freedom of the Children of God

The resurrection life must be characterised by freedom. By that, I most emphatically do not mean that it is impossible to be people of resurrection faith except in a free society. Very often, indeed, a 'free' society is where people seem to find it most difficult, as I have tried to suggest earlier. I refer to an inner freedom which shows itself in remarkable outward living. Perhaps it would be easiest to describe this by presenting a hypothetical situation.

Suppose for a moment that the risen Jesus had come face to face with the people who had brought about his death. There is room for much fruitful speculation here, but I propose to concentrate upon one aspect. Let us then suppose that, having recovered from their shock, they had attempted to keep Jesus quiet by threats. I have a delightful mental image of Jesus saying to Caiaphas or to Pilate, 'What are you going to do – kill me again? It didn't work last time!' I happen to believe, with regard to the crucifixion, that Jesus died in faith with no actual *knowledge* of what the outcome would be, a belief underpinned by the reasoning contained in the preceding chapters. However, having once gone through that barrier, he would have been able to face whatever other threats were brought with a sense of real freedom. No lingering doubts now; death is known not to be a threat. The sense of liberation would have been indescribable.

Now I do not suggest that we have *that* kind of certainty; it was not we who went through that experience. We might, though, consider again the dramatic change which happened in the disciples, whose entire lives were transformed. In them we see people whose attitude to death does seem to have undergone a radical transformation of the kind I have suggested. For all of us, death is still an unknown and the resurrection of Jesus does not give us any special knowledge, but it does give us the basis for *faith*. It gives us something on which we can base our commitment to live the radically new life of the kingdom of God right in the middle of 'Galilee' or

'Jerusalem', so that our lives may be a sign of hope. They may also be a powerful protest against all that is life-denying: all that enables futility to masquerade as hope, and the nightmare of hyped-up greed as a romantic dream; all that presents the death-bound existence of a sick culture as the fullness of life.

That, of course, is a risky business. We might end up – from a material point of view – poorer, less secure; we might be less well liked by respectable society; we might sometimes find ourselves in threatening situations; we might find that the very people from whom we expected support either turn against us or simply desert us when we get to our Gethsemane. But we live on the other side of Easter. We are people of resurrection faith. We have 'seen Life'! We have walked with one who faced all of that and remained true to the values of the kingdom of God. And we have encountered him, risen and triumphant, with the assurance that we may follow where he has gone before. All of which makes the life of the church as it is generally viewed somewhat puzzling.

When David Jenkins raised the old issues of the nature of resurrection, and was deliberately misrepresented for the sake of sensationalism, many people made ecclesiastical capital out of vaunting their 'correct' doctrine and claiming to 'believe in the resurrection'. The whole Christian community, it seemed, was desperate to make it publicly clear that its belief in the risen Christ was unshakeable. That being so, we must ask why the life of the church is not more clearly characterised by that belief. Why does the church so often fail to stand out as radically distinctive, not because of what it says but the way it lives? Now it should be said here that there are Christian communities in this country and elsewhere which very definitely do that; Iona and Corrymeela spring readily to mind, and there are many local congregations which in one way or other take the risks of resurrection faith. However, it must be said that the general impression one has is that the 'body of Christ on earth' is desperately trying to hang onto its life, afraid of losing it and sad at having already lost a large measure of the worldly wealth and status which once it had. At national level, the church seems remote from the people among whom Christ lived and still lives; and at local level it appears to be hung up on ensuring its survival either by raising funds or by filling its pews and hopefully therefore its coffers. In some cases the identity of the church as the body of Christ on earth has become almost completely obscured by its new identity as a pillar of the status quo and – too often – a preserver of ancient monuments as the energy, creativity and sheer love of good people is diverted from the things of the kingdom and devoted to fund raising activities in order to pay for the next round of repairs. Now I do not say that beautiful monuments should not be preserved, but I fail to see any theological argument that it is the church's responsibility to do it.

Many of the sayings of Jesus are too easily applied only to individuals, and their relevance to the church as a body is overlooked. This is unjustifiable when so many of them were addressed to the disciples as a whole rather than to individuals. The following text is an example of this.

> For those who want to save their life will lose it, and those who lose their life for my sake will find it. For what will it profit them if they gain the whole world but forfeit their life? Or what will they give in return for their life?[95]

For us who live in relatively safe places, of course, it is much less threatening if we simply take it literally and relate it to individual lives; the danger of our actually being asked to die for our faith is remote in the extreme. When it comes to churches as institutions, however, it is a different matter. While it is true that some churches take great risks in faith, they are regrettably a tiny minority. Our towns and villages are full of churches struggling to survive; seeking to save their

[95] Mat 16:25-26

own lives. Faced with declining congregations and rising costs, they begin to husband their resources. A catchphrase of a local church leader I once knew was, 'We don't want to lose anybody'. The whole life of the church was geared to hanging onto what – and whom – they had. This is certainly true of many many congregations. The policy is of survival. Do not offend people, do not ask awkward questions, and cost every initiative very carefully before embarking upon it. As a result churches are dying slowly and painfully with little possibility of resurrection, for they are seeking to save their own lives. Let the church take the risk Jesus took of being radically distinctive; of being prepared to dump religiosity in favour of true religion; of getting involved with people and issues which society wants kept hidden. People will be offended; many will leave the churches; those who consider themselves good will say we are breaking the rules and undermining society. Well, Jesus said that whatever people did to him they would do to his followers. Let us then rejoice in slander and calumny because it is a sign that we are truly following Jesus. And let us do so in true resurrection faith, believing that as we risk our 'life' for the sake of the kingdom we shall find life in all its fullness in Christ.

Many very good practical arguments can be advanced in favour of the present attitudes, of course, not least that the church must survive if it is to continue to spread the gospel – and it is that very argument (and the fact that it is found to be so convincing) which reveals the lack of true resurrection faith. The same argument could well have been used by Christ when standing before Pilate. No doubt it occurred to him. Yet, at the age of thirty or so, he was prepared to lose everything, including his own life, rather than be unfaithful to his mission. He died in faith, with no absolute guarantee or certainty that his death would not be the end of everything he stood for. It was a risk he had to take and it is a risk the church has to take as well.

There is a legend about Christ arriving in heaven after his ascension and being met by Gabriel who asked, 'What provision have you made for the continuing of your work?'

Christ replied, 'I have left a dozen friends to continue it.' With a quizzical look, Gabriel asked, 'And if that fails what alternative provision have you made?' to which Christ simply replied, 'There is no alternative provision.' The whole mission of Christ was put at risk and then entrusted to people of the most slender resources. No back-up system in case of failure, no reserve of funds or weapons just in case things did not work out. And all of that from the wrong side of Easter! We are on the 'right' side of Easter. We believe in resurrection; we have encountered the risen Christ. What then should we fear? Let us live the life of the world to come, here in this world, and face the cost of that in resurrection faith! Let us open our lives and our communities to the people whom we find threatening or embarrassing, and take the risk of not seeking to save our church's lives but offer them to God in the faith that if they appear to be 'lost' he will turn the loss into creative possibility.

We speak a great deal of 'offering things to God'. Where is this God to whom we offer our lives and our resources? In a building that must be preserved? In the creeds and dogmas which must be defended at all costs (well, most costs, anyway)? Where were the disciples told to go and look for the risen Christ?

'There you will see him.'

> But he said to them, 'Do not be alarmed; you are looking for Jesus of Nazareth, who was crucified. He has been raised; he is not here. Look, there is the place they laid him. But go, tell his disciples and Peter that he is going ahead of you to Galilee; there you will see him, just as he told you.'[96]

So often, we seem to think we have to take Christ to people. The message to the disciples was crystal clear: he is already out in the world ahead of us. Once again, we find ourselves called to 'go back' – back to the place of mission,

[96] Mark 16:6-7

where there has already been misunderstanding, hostility and pain. That is where we shall find the risen Christ. He does not wait for us in the empty tomb – or in any other large, empty and obsolete building! Although there are now at least two sites claimed to be the original tomb in Jerusalem, and the tourist industry does very well out of them, we must remember that the disciples were directed away from the empty (and redundant) tomb to where they would actually encounter the risen Christ – out in the world.

Some years ago I questioned the practice of holding processions of witness around the neighbourhood. My reasons for that can be left perhaps for another time or another book; what was significant was the reply which I received: 'What you say might well be right, but *that is the only time those people see us.*' I wonder whether Jesus would have had the impact he did if the only time people had seen him had been when he was engaged in a publicity exercise! Where, I wondered, on that present day housing estate, was the local body of Christ when his people (which includes everyone) were worrying about their mortgages, caring for their sick and dying, standing in queues in benefit offices, stretching the family budget to breaking point, sweating at the factory or swearing at the car battery?

As I indicated earlier, there are churches who are involved; churches which devote their resources of money, energy and most of all faith to the people around them and the wholeness of the wider creation. If we were to attend one of those churches on Easter Sunday we should be unlikely to hear in the sermon a discussion of the empty tomb or the metaphysics of a bodily resurrection. We should be far more likely to hear the voice of those who had truly encountered the risen Christ where he is most readily to be found: Go back to 'Galilee'. There you will find him.

God among the people. 'God in us' if you like.

Not in control.

In relationship.

Bibliography

Principal Works Cited

Dietrich Bonhoeffer: *Life Together* (SCM 1985)

Alastair V. Campbell: *The Gospel of Anger* (SPCK 1986)

Don Cupitt: *Christ and the Hiddenness of God* (SCM 1985)

Paul S. Fiddes: *Past Event and Present Salvation* (DLT 1989)

Gustavo Gutierrez: *The Power of the Poor in History* (SCM 1983)

Gerard Hughes: *God of Surprises* (DLT 1985)

Klaus Koch: *The Prophets. Vol. 1* (SCM 1982)

Hans Kung: *Eternal Life?* (Collins 1984)

John Macquarrie: *Principles of Christian Theology* (SCM 1986)

Jurgen Moltmann: *God in Creation* (SCM 1985)

Henri J. M Nouwen: *The Return of the Prodigal Son* (DLT 1994)

Ruth Page: *The Incarnation of Freedom and Love* (SCM 1991)

John Polkinghorne: *Science and Christian Belief* (SPCK 1994)

G. A. Studdert Kennedy: *Rhymes* (Hodder and Stoughton 1932)

J.R.R. Tolkien: *The Hobbit*

John D. Weaver: *In the Beginning God* (Regent's Study Guides: Regent's Park College, Oxford & Smyth and Helwys, Georgia, USA., 1994)

Frances Young: *Sacrifice and the Death of Christ* (SCM 1983)

Suggestions For Further Reading

By no means an exhaustive list, but it might enable some of the discussions in this book to be pursued further.

Eric Blakebrough: *Permission to Be* (DLT 1992)

F. W. Dillistone: *The Christian Understanding of Atonement* (SCM 1984)

Paul S. Fiddes: *The Creative Suffering of God* (OUP 1989)

Mary Grey: *Redeeming the Dream [Feminism, Redemption and Christian Tradition]* (SPCK 1989)

Gustavo Gutierrez: *A Theology of Liberation* (SCM 1988)

Gustavo Gutierrez: *We Drink from Our Own Wells* (SCM 1984)

Hanson & Hanson: *Reasonable Belief* (OUP 1987)

Margaret Hebblethwaite: *Motherhood and God* (Chapman 1984)

David Jenkins: *The Glory of Man* (SCM 1984)

David & Rebecca Jenkins: *Free to Believe* (BBC 1991)

Christopher B. Kaiser: *The Doctrine of God* (Marshall, Morgan and Scott 1982)

Hans Kung: *On Being a Christian* (Collins 1986)

Kenneth Leech: *True Prayer* (Sheldon 1986)

Frances Makower: *Faith or Folly? [Drugs, Ministry and Community]* (DLT 1989)

Alwyn Marriage: *Life-Giving Spirit [Responding to the Feminine in God]* (SPCK 1989)

Thomas Merton: *Contemplative Prayer* (DLT 1985)

Jurgen Moltmann: *God in Creation [An Ecological Doctrine of Creation]* (SCM 1985)

Jurgen Moltmann: *The Open Church [Invitation to a Messianic Lifestyle]* (SCM 1978)

Jurgen Moltmann & Elizabeth Moltmann-Wendel: *Humanity in God* (SCM 1983)

General Index

M

N

INDEX OF BIBLICAL REFERENCES

INDEX OF BIBLICAL CHARACTERS

Index of Non-Biblical Names

INDEX OF ANALOGIES AND ILLUSTRATIONS